I AM THE STORM

by

Krisi Rodriguez

Library of Congress Control Number (LCCN): 2026905825

ISBNs:
eBook: 979-8-90224-148-5
Paperback: 979-8-90224-149-2
Hardback: 979-8-90224-151-5

Published by:
Authors Publishing House
178 Broadway, 3rd Floor, #1343
New York, NY 10001, USA

Main Line: (855) 624-0155
Email: support@authorspublishinghouse.com

Table of Contents

Preface 1

Part 1: Defining 3

Section 1: The Storm Begins to Gather................................4

Chapter 1: The Rules for Being a Girl 5

Chapter 2: When the Family Splits....................................11

Chapter 3: The Father, Unbound 15

Chapter 4: No Safe Adults...18

Section 2: Lessons in Life 24

Chapter 5: When Harm Becomes Familiar 25

Chapter 6: The Architecture of Silence.............................30

Chapter 7: Triggers Revealed 37

Part 1 Summary 43

Part 2: Stirring the Storm 44

Section 1: Love 45

Chapter 8: First Love, First Lessons 46

Chapter 9: Lover, Protector, Womanizer 52

Chapter 10: Entertain Me but Don't Love Me....................56

Chapter 11: Love as Control.......................................61

Section 2: Marriage 71

Chapter 12: Carrying the Weight 72

Chapter 13: When Pressure Masquerades as Love 80

Section 3: Lessons Learned 91

Chapter 14: How to Say No (When You Were Never Taught) 92

Part 2: Summary 99

Part 3 : Awakening the Storm 100

Chapter 15: The Door That Closed 101

Chapter 16: A Betrayal in Writing 108

Chapter 17: The Price of Boundaries 118

Chapter 18: The Early Arrival of Grief 126

Part 3: Summary 137

Part 4: Becoming the Storm 138

Chapter 19: When Someone Finally Sees You...........................139

Chapter 20: Motherhood, Rewritten...................................148

Chapter 22: Breaking the Mold......................................165

Part 4: Summary...175

A Letter: To the Woman Still Navigating the Weather 176

The Healing Earth..184

Resources: Parenting is Hard 185

Preface

Can you remember your first memory?

I'm not talking about the stories people tell you about yourself, the ones that get repeated so many times they start to feel like memories, even though you don't actually remember being there. I mean the first real memory. The first time you weren't watching yourself in a story, but were actually *in* the scene, moving, noticing, absorbing the world around you.

My first real memory was in kindergarten.

We were sitting in a little circle on the floor, legs crossed, hands in our laps, the room buzzing with the soft chaos only five-year-olds can create. Then a girl next to me sneezed. A small thing. Ordinary. But she lifted her hands to her face, cupped them over her nose and mouth, and then calmly stood up to get a tissue.

I remember staring at her, frozen with a strange kind of awareness.

Should I do that? Am I doing it wrong? Is there a better way to be?

I had never questioned something so small before, but suddenly I was hyper-aware of myself in relation to her. My instinct wasn't, "She sneezed." It was, "Should I be more like her?" That moment, that tiny sneeze, was the beginning of something I didn't understand until much later.

It set the stage for my whole life.

Always comparing.

Always adjusting.

Always measuring myself against others, not just in my own mind, but in a world constantly measuring me too.

Part 1: Defining

Before the storm breaks, the sky doesn't scream.

It darkens.

It thickens.

The air grows heavy with what hasn't yet been said.

Here, the storm was still quiet.

Still building.

Still waiting for its name.

Section 1: The Storm Begins to Gather

Pressure

It is the first drop of pressure.

The first cloud forming where the sky used to be clear.

The first whisper of weather no one taught you to name.

It's gathering:

The storm did not begin with thunder.

It began with the quiet, relentless pressure

of learning that no one is coming to keep you safe.

Love is conditional.

Your body is always being watched.

Your voice is something to swallow.

This is where the pressure starts to build.

Not in the world outside, but in the small, fierce, terrified heart of a girl who is already learning to become the weather,

because the sky above offers no shelter.

Chapter 1: The Rules for Being a Girl

After that kindergarten moment with the sneeze, I began to notice there was a "right way" to do things.

A right way to sit.

A right way to speak.

A right way to behave.

And every time I didn't quite match it, I felt the invisible nudge of correction - sometimes through a look, sometimes through a comment, and sometimes through silence.

I didn't have the language for it then, but I was beginning to understand girls learned who they were by constant comparison.

Am I doing this right?

Am I good enough?

Am I what they expect?

And "they" could be anyone: parents, teachers, boys, other girls, strangers.

There are rules for being a girl.

No one hands them to you.

No one sits you down and explains them.

But they seep into you anyway, quietly, subtly, invisibly, until one day you realize you've been following them your whole life without even knowing you learned them.

By elementary school, the rules were already forming.

Be polite.

Be sweet.

Don't be too loud.

Don't be too rough.

Smile.

Don't take up too much space.

Say thank you even when you don't feel it.

And above all, *don't make anyone uncomfortable*.

What no one tells you is this last rule becomes a trap, because one day, you start sacrificing your own comfort just to maintain someone else's. That's when the lines blur. That's when harm hides itself inside expectations.

But back then, I just wanted to be the kind of girl teachers liked.

The kind of girl who didn't get in trouble.

The kind of girl who made adults smile approvingly and boys leave her alone, and other girls invite her to paint with them during free time.

I didn't realize how early the molding begins.

When I think back, I can see the small moments that stitched themselves into who I believed I had to be.

When a teacher said, "Boys will be boys," and I learned girls were supposed to tolerate what boys got away with.

When a family member said, "Sit like a lady," I learned my body was always being watched.

When adults praised me for being quiet and obedient, I learned my needs were secondary to my behavior.

These weren't dramatic, life-changing incidents. They were subtle, repeated lessons soaked into me before I ever had a chance to question them.

And that's the thing about conditioning;

it doesn't feel like conditioning while it's happening.

It feels like normal.

Like belonging.

Like survival.

No one warns you that one day, these quiet little rules can grow into something heavier. Something that shapes how you handle pressure, how you respond to danger, how you interpret manipulation, and how you navigate spaces where your voice is the only thing that could save you, but you've spent years learning not to use it.

The Insult

When I was young, life seemed good on the surface. I had an older sister, a year older than I, and when we were little, we were inseparable. We played, laughed, fought in small ways, and made up just as quickly. There was a sweetness to those early years, making me believe this was what life would always be like, simple, safe, full of music.

I remember riding through the Ohio Amish country with my mom, her friend, and all of us girls piled in the car. The Footloose soundtrack was blaring, the windows were down, and we were all singing loud and off-key, but joyfully. I was eight-ish. I felt free. I felt part of something.

Until I wasn't.

My mom turned to me, in front of everyone, and said,

"Stop singing. You sound horrible."

The other girls kept singing. They were welcomed in the moment.

I was shut out of it. I was singled out. I was embarrassed.

What I heard wasn't "don't sing."

I heard:

you are less than,

you are embarrassing,

you don't fit,

mute yourself.

My cheeks burned. My chest tightened. My voice retreated somewhere deep inside my bones, where it would stay locked away for years. I didn't sing in front of another person until adulthood. One comment, one moment, became a lifetime of self-doubt.

I absorbed the message long before I understood it.

Your feelings are inconvenient.

Your pain is excessive.

Your voice is unwanted.

These small lessons accumulate.

And so, I learned to swallow my emotions whole.

To hold myself tightly.

To disappear on command.

But something else was happening too, something more dangerous. Silence wasn't just expected; it was rewarded. When I was quiet, I was "good."

When I didn't complain, I was "easy."

When I didn't cry or question or resist, adults smiled.

Approval felt like love, and so I chased it the only way I knew how - by minimizing myself.

I didn't know then learning to silence myself was going to shape everything that came later, every relationship, every danger I didn't know how to name, every boundary I didn't know how to set.

The rules were simple:

   don't cry,

   don't speak,

   don't resist.

But as I grew older, the rules got heavier.

More complicated.

More harmful.

And eventually… they became impossible to follow.

Chapter 2: When the Family Splits

Families don't fall apart all at once.

They first split in small ways: a shift in tone, a strange tension, a routine suddenly changes.

When you're a child, you don't recognize these as warning signs.

You just know something in the air feels different.

At first, my family still looked normal from the outside.

Two parents.

Two daughters.

A house.

A routine.

But the cracks began forming quietly, in the spaces between what adults said and what they did.

Before my parents divorced, my mom and her friend started hanging out every weekend. For my sister and me, it felt like an adventure. We stayed at the friend's apartment, watched TV, slept on the floor in sleeping bags, and giggled into the night. It felt like freedom, a break from the rules, a break from normal.

But under that excitement, something was shifting.

Those weekends away weren't about us.

They were about my mother leaving the marriage one Saturday at a time.

As children, we didn't see it.

But as an adult, I can look back and recognize those were the first signs that home wasn't as safe or stable as I thought. We weren't being "treated to fun weekends."

We were being moved out of the way.

And while my mother drifted outward, my father began changing in ways I didn't understand. Conversations and behaviors were introduced that no child should have to navigate, things confusing, inappropriate, and framed as normal. When you grow up in an environment where adults treat the strange as ordinary, you learn to doubt your instincts. You begin to believe the world is shaped this way everywhere.

It wasn't.

But I didn't know that then.

The day the divorce became real is burned into my memory.

It was the Christmas season.

A day that should feel warm and safe and filled with magic.

Instead, I walked into the house knowing my dad was gone… and it felt like loneliness seeped into every corner of my skin.

Children don't have words for grief like that.

They just feel the world go quiet in a way that feels wrong.

But the deepest crack, the one that split me in two, came after the divorce.

When my parents separated, most children live with their mother by default. That's what I expected. That's what felt safe. That's what made sense.

Instead, my mother decided my father would raise us.

I remember begging her not to do it.

Begging her to let us stay.

Begging her to choose us.

She said he was "better educated," that he could "help with school," that she would be "working," that it made "more sense."

But none of that was true.

He wasn't better; he was just available.

And she wanted to be free.

Her choice wasn't about our well-being. It was about her freedom.

I didn't have the ability or the safety to tell her what was really happening in our home.

I couldn't say the things no child should have to say.

I couldn't risk sending my father to jail.

He was still my dad.

So, I said nothing.

And we stayed with him.

Childhood shouldn't require that kind of silence.

It shouldn't require that kind of sacrifice.

That moment, standing in front of my mother, begging not to be left behind, was a fracture that never fully healed. It wasn't just a custody decision. It was confirmation of something I had been slowly learning my entire life.

You cannot depend on the people who are supposed to protect you.

You cannot assume adults will put your safety first.

The little girl who learned not to cry was now learning not to expect anything either.

These early cracks didn't just split my family; they split my identity.

They made me feel unanchored.

Untethered.

Unworthy of stability.

And when a child feels unworthy, the world becomes a place you navigate carefully, always watching, always adjusting, always bracing for the next shift.

The storm inside me didn't start with something loud.

It started with a quiet realization.

Home wasn't safe.

Love wasn't reliable.

And childhood wasn't a place I could stay.

Chapter 3: The Father, Unbound

My father was complicated.

He wasn't just one thing, not a single-note villain, and not a safe haven either.

He was a mixture of charm, humor, unpredictability, loneliness, and a deep hunger for attention he didn't know how to get in healthy ways.

And when you're a child, you don't understand contradictions.

You just absorb them.

There were moments when he acted like the kind of dad little girls dream about.

He coached softball teams.

He fixed our scrapes.

He bought the newest gadgets, the first VHS player, the first home computer, making our house the destination for every kid in the neighborhood.

He made us feel like our home was exciting, modern, special.

But beneath those shiny moments was a darker undercurrent, one I didn't have the language for then.

A father might be funny, involved, or generous... yet also unpredictable, boundaryless, and emotionally unsafe.

That was my father.

He changed sharply when my parents divorced.

It was as if the floor fell out from under him, and he didn't know how to stand. He was hurting, lonely, angry. Instead of seeking help or support, he pulled his daughters into the emotional vacuum left behind.

He became too familiar, too unfiltered, too reliant on us to fill the space that an adult partner would normally occupy.

And the burden of that, the emotional weight of becoming what a parent needs, is crushing for a child.

He blurred roles constantly.

One minute, he was the fun, playful dad who brought home pizza and movies; the next, he was someone we didn't quite recognize. Someone who shared things no father should share with a child. Someone who used adult language and adult themes as if we were his peers, not his daughters. Someone who treated boundaries like suggestions.

When adults normalize things, children follow their lead.

So my sister and I believed this was what life looked like, what homes looked like, what fathers were like.

We didn't know our reality was off-center.

We didn't know it was strange.

We didn't know it was unsafe.

We just thought it was ours.

My dad became the center of our world, a world confusing, inconsistent, emotionally volatile, and without the safety rails most children take for granted.

He shaped me in ways that took decades to unlearn.

He shaped my understanding of what love looks like.

He shaped my instinct to internalize discomfort rather than name it.

He shaped my silence, my people-pleasing, my tolerance for chaos.

He shaped the storm inside me long before I knew I carried it.

He was the first person to teach me adults can fail you completely and still expect your loyalty.

He was the first person to teach me how power can be used in ways leaving no visible mark but still change the shape of who you become.

And he was the first person to teach me something I needed to unlearn to survive - your feelings don't matter if someone else needs you more.

My father didn't create the storm.

But he stirred it.

He fed it.

He sharpened its edges.

And later, much later, his impact became the very force I would rise against when I decided I would no longer be silent, small, or controlled by the weather around me.

Chapter 4: No Safe Adults

There is a particular kind of loneliness that happens when you grow up surrounded by adults but never actually protected by them.

It isn't quiet or gentle.

It is sharp.

It teaches you to scan the room before speaking.

It teaches you to read people before you read yourself.

It teaches you safety is something you create, not something you receive.

My childhood was full of adults: parents, relatives, coaches, neighbors. Yet very few of them acted like guardians. They were there, physically, moving through the same spaces I occupied, but there was an emotional and moral absence, leaving me to navigate life without the anchors children should have.

I learned early:

adults can be present and still not be safe,

adults can love you and still fail you,

adults can be in the room and still leave you alone.

The adults in my life became even more unpredictable. My mother drifted toward her freedom and away from child-rearing responsibility.

My father filled the empty air with noise, sometimes entertaining, sometimes confusing, sometimes deeply unsettling, always unstable.

Children don't have the words "boundary," "inappropriate," or "unsafe."

Children only have feelings, and mine were a tangle of confusion, discomfort, and forced maturity.

There were moments I desperately wanted someone to see us. Really see us. To realize two young girls were absorbing the emotional chaos of adults who were lost themselves. But no one stepped in. No one asked questions. No one looked close enough to notice the shape of our childhood wasn't normal.

Instead, the message was clear.

Keep quiet.

Carry it.

Get through it.

It wasn't just my parents who failed to protect us.

Other adults did too.

I remember one summer day when my aunts came to visit. I was in the living room chatting with them when the tension in the house shifted, the kind of shift you learn to feel even before you can describe it. My dad was angry my sister wasn't cleaning her room fast enough. He grabbed the fraternity paddle he used for punishment and marched upstairs.

I tried to talk louder, to drown out whatever was coming, but my sister's scream broke through everything. It was the kind of scream that stops the world. My insides disappeared. My body turned cold.

I excused myself to check on her, heart pounding, legs shaking.

But my father stopped me at the stairs, turned me around, told me to go back.

And I went.

I sat there.

With my aunts.

In the thickest silence I have ever felt.

Two adult women, aunts, our family. They heard her scream and did nothing. They left soon after, without checking on her, without asking questions, without intervening.

That day taught me as much about adults as my parents ever did.

Some people will hear your pain and still choose silence.

Some people will witness harm and walk away.

Some people will protect their comfort before they ever protect a child.

I did not have adults who created safety. I had adults who created instability.

I had adults who explained away their choices and ignored their responsibilities.

I had adults who taught me suffering is private and help is optional.

And yet, through all of this, I didn't see myself as unsafe.

I saw myself as responsible.

Responsible for keeping the peace.

Responsible for staying out of the way.

Responsible for adjusting, fixing, absorbing.

When children are forced to grow up inside chaos, they don't become wild.

They become disciplined.

Hyperaware.

Quiet.

Performative.

Strong in the ways of masking the breaking underneath.

I carried the weight of adults who never carried me.

I learned to make myself invisible to avoid being hurt.

I learned to anticipate moods to avoid being punished.

I learned to swallow fear because there was no one to tell it to.

Children who grow up without safety become exceptionally good at emotional labor.

They become the fixers.

The peacekeepers.

The ones who make everyone else comfortable, even when they are hurting.

The ones who present strength because breaking is not an option.

Sometimes people mistake this for resilience.

But resilience forged through survival is not the same as resilience forged through support.

One grows upward. But the other grows inward.

And inward is where I lived for years, in my mind, in my imagination, in silence, in the small space I carved out for myself where nothing could hurt me because no one could reach me.

That internal world became my refuge.

My shadow armor.

My secret strength.

It also became the place where my storm began to gather, quietly at first, like a shift in air pressure. Then, more forcefully, as the years went on and the cracks in my family deepened.

The adults around me didn't see the storm forming inside me. They didn't see the child growing up too fast, teaching herself emotional survival without a guide, learning love was conditional, and safety was inconsistent.

And because I had no model for healthy boundaries or emotional expression, I learned to internalize everything. Hurt became something I swallowed. Fear became something I hid. Confusion became a quiet layer under my skin. Loneliness became something I carried without words.

Section 2: Lessons in Life

Thunder

The storm forming inside me wasn't anger;

> It was all the words I never said, all the emotions I never expressed, all the truths I was never allowed to speak.

And storms don't stay silent forever.

Something was coming.

> An awakening,
>
> A breaking open,
>
> A reckoning.

Chapter 5: When Harm Becomes Familiar

Children don't know what's normal. They only know what's familiar.

And what is familiar becomes the blueprint for how you understand the world.

When I look back now, I can see so clearly how many things in my childhood were wrong emotionally, psychologically, developmentally. But at the time, I didn't know they were wrong.

I thought they were normal.

I thought everyone lived this way.

I thought this was just "family."

That is the danger of growing up in an environment where boundaries don't exist, and adults don't protect you.

Harm hides itself by becoming routine.

When children grow up thinking harm is normal.

They grow into teenagers and adults who:

don't trust their instincts,

doubt their discomfort,

ignore red flags,

endure inappropriate behavior,

minimize their own feelings,

stay quiet when they should speak,

accept treatment they shouldn't,

struggle to define boundaries because they never learned any.

Your body feels something is wrong,

but your brain has been trained not to believe it.

This is how harmful environments replicate themselves,

long after you've left the house where they began.

As I grew, I started to see, to become aware.

It wasn't one moment, it was a series of small shocks.

Going to friends' houses and noticing the quiet stability.

Watching parents interact without tension.

Seeing boundaries respected.

Seeing families sit together without an undercurrent of discomfort.

The contrast was startling, unsettling, and confusing.

Part of me felt jealous.

Part of me felt angry.

Part of me felt like an outsider.

Part of me didn't trust it. Stability felt too foreign to believe.

Awareness is painful, but it's also the beginning of power.

But, this is where little cracks of realization started forming.

Maybe this isn't normal.

Maybe not everyone lives like this.

Maybe children aren't supposed to feel this unsafe.

Maybe something is wrong here,

I began to understand the foundation of my life had been built on distortions.

And once you see the distortion,

> even a little bit,

> you can't unsee it.

You begin the slow, long, painful journey of untangling:

> what is normal, from what is familiar,

> what is safe, from what is routine,

> what is love, from what is dysfunction.

This is where my storm learned its first truth:

> *Just because something feels normal doesn't mean it's right.*

Where innocence started to dissolve.

Where silence took deeper root.

Where I began to grow up too fast.

It explains how I eventually became the storm.

Shaped by the cracks,

Strengthened by the fractures,

Forged in the places where protection should have been but wasn't.

These were the beginnings of the storm inside me;

a storm built not from rebellion,

but from survival.

Emotional survival in a child is recognizable.

You smile more than you feel.

You hide more than you show.

You talk carefully, cautiously.

You become pleasing. Not because you want to, but because it keeps you safe.

You learn to be "easy" because difficult children don't survive environments like this.

And though I didn't know it then, every moment of survival was shaping the woman I would eventually become:

strong,

self-reliant,

emotionally intuitive,

resilient beyond measure…

and hungry for a life where safety wasn't a privilege but a right.

This chapter of my life didn't make me weak.

It made me weather-resistant.

Because storms don't form all at once.

This was only the beginning.

This shaped the woman I would become.

It sharpened my intuition.

It strengthened my instincts.

It made me hyper-aware, empathetic, observant.

It taught me how to survive any emotional climate.

But it also planted the seeds for something else, something powerful:

The understanding that I wanted more. I deserved more.

Chapter 6: The Architecture of Silence

Silence isn't empty.

It's full. It's full of everything you didn't say, everything you held back, everything you were too afraid to admit even to yourself. Silence is not just the absence of words.

For children like me, silence becomes a way of living.

Silence became my shield.

Silence became my strategy.

Silence became my identity.

When you grow up learning to protect adults from your feelings, you don't develop emotional freedom. You develop emotional triggers, raw, reactive points inside you formed in childhood, pressed again and again until they become part of your nervous system.

Triggers are not flaws.

They're unhealed alarms.

They're warnings from the child you once were.. The child who had to survive without help.

I didn't know that then.

I only knew the world made me flinch in places other kids didn't.

By the time I reached adolescence, I had already become fluent in the language of quiet self-protection, a language you learn when speaking up only makes things worse, when your feelings are dismissed, when danger is disguised as normal, and when the people who should have protected you instead protected their comfort.

When you grow up learning your voice is either ignored or punished, silence feels like safety.

Until it doesn't.

Silence started as survival.

Silence meant:

    don't cry, it won't change anything,

    don't ask, the answer will hurt,

    don't question, adults don't like that,

    don't upset the balance, it's already fragile.

I learned early speaking up could create conflict, and conflict usually meant consequences. So, I swallowed my words. I hid what I knew. I hid what I feared. I hid what I felt.

Silence kept me from being targeted.

Silence kept me from making situations worse.

Silence kept me safe, or at least, that's what I told myself.

But survival skills protecting children often harm adults.

By middle school, I didn't just choose silence — I became it.

I didn't argue.

I didn't complain.

I didn't cry.

I didn't reveal pain.

I didn't reveal fear.

I didn't reveal confusion.

Even with friends, I stayed agreeable.

Even with teachers, I stayed compliant.

Even with myself, I stayed quiet.

I thought this made me strong.

But silence isn't strength, it's containment.

And contained pain doesn't disappear.

It hardens.

It deepens.

It calcifies inside you.

Children are not supposed to carry adult-sized secrets or adult-sized emotions.

But I did.

And I learned to carry them without making a sound.

Everywhere I turned, the message was the same.

Your feelings are not welcome here.

Your truth is not convenient.

Your voice makes people uncomfortable.

And when things hurt, when things were wrong, when things were frightening or confusing…

I stayed silent.

Not because I didn't feel anything,

but because I felt everything, and had nowhere to put it.

Silence was the only container I had.

The cost of silence doesn't show up immediately.

It doesn't hit all at once.

Silence shows up later:

in the relationships you choose,

in the boundaries you don't set,

in the danger you don't avoid,

in the red flags you rationalize,

in the way you tolerate what should never be tolerated.

Silence teaches you:

to accept less than you need,

to endure more than you should,

to question your instincts,

to doubt your discomfort,

to think pain is normal,

and to believe your voice will only make things worse.

Silence prepares you to survive childhood…

…but it leaves you unequipped to protect yourself in adolescence and adulthood.

And that is the real cost.

There comes a moment in every survivor's life when silence stops being a shield and becomes a trap.

For me, that shift happened slowly, subtly, not in one moment, but in the accumulation of many.

Moments when I didn't speak up, even when something felt wrong.

Moments when I tolerated things I didn't want because I didn't know I was allowed to say no.

Moments when I let other people's needs overtake my own, because that was all I had ever known.

Moments when danger slipped under the radar because I had been trained to doubt myself.

Silence didn't keep me safe.

Silence kept me compliant.

And compliance is not safety. It is invisibility.

I didn't know how to use my voice.

I didn't know what it meant to advocate for myself.

I didn't know how to draw boundaries.

I didn't know "no" was an option.

I didn't know my feelings had value.

I only knew how to endure.

People saw me as strong.

Resilient.

Capable.

Independent.

Mature for my age.

But they weren't seeing strength.

They were seeing survival.

They were seeing a girl who had been conditioned not to break down.

Who had been trained to hold everything inside.

Who had been taught vulnerability was a liability.

Who had been shaped by adults who didn't show her what comfort looked like.

Silence becomes a second skin.

You wear it everywhere.

You don't know who you are without it.

But silence also hides your inner world so effectively that sometimes even you forget to listen to it.

It took me years to understand silence wasn't protection; it was suppression.

And suppression has a cost.

A muted voice.

A blurred identity.

A lifetime of carrying emotions in secret.

And relationships built on endurance instead of mutual understanding.

Silence teaches your body to react before your mind understands.

Silence is not passive.

It's architecture.

Silence keeps you safe as a child.

But as an adult, it becomes a prison.

And every emotional trigger is a reminder.

There are parts of you still waiting to be heard.

Still waiting to be seen.

Still waiting to be healed.

A moment when silence would no longer be the safest option.

Chapter 7: Triggers Revealed

My emotional triggers began forming long before I knew what the word meant.

Over time, I began to understand.

My triggers weren't signs of brokenness; they were signs of a woman who had survived what should have destroyed her.

Trigger 1: Raised Voices

A tone shift.

A slammed door.

A quick inhale before someone speaks.

Even the slightest change in volume could send my mind scanning for danger.

Is someone angry?

Did I do something wrong?

Do I need to disappear?

My body responded before I could think - tightening, freezing, bracing.

This is what hypervigilance looks like in a child.

Trigger 2: Being Told "Stop Crying"

As a child, crying brought annoyance, not comfort.

Grief brought impatience, not arms around me.

So as an adult, tears became shameful.

When emotions rose, I shut them down.

When someone tried to comfort me, I stiffened.

When I cried alone, I felt guilt instead of release.

I didn't learn emotional regulation; I learned emotional suppression.

Trigger 3: Being Ignored or Unheard

Growing up, my voice often didn't matter.

My words didn't change outcomes.

My feelings didn't influence decisions.

So later in life, when someone interrupted me, dismissed me, or talked over me, it didn't just annoy me,

    it hit the same wound from childhood.

You don't matter.

Your voice isn't important.

Stay quiet.

These weren't new feelings; they were echoes.

Trigger 4: Sudden Kindness

This one took years to understand.

When someone praised me, offered help, or showed unexpected gentleness, I felt uneasy.

Suspicious.

Waiting for the shift.

Waiting for the moment kindness turned into control or disappointment.

Because in childhood, affection was inconsistent.

Warm one moment, cold the next.

Loving one day, unreachable the next.

Kindness didn't feel safe. It felt like the beginning of a trap.

Compliments were bad words.

Empty.

Manipulative.

There was something they wanted, and I just waited for that to surface.

Trigger 5: Being Needed Too Much

As a child, I learned how to carry the emotional weight of adults.

I was the fixer.

The good girl.

The one who knew how to adjust herself to keep the peace.

So later, when someone depended on me heavily, in love, at work, in friendships, it triggered panic.

Not because I didn't care.

But because I had lived a lifetime of over-functioning before I even reached adulthood.

Triggers showed up later in life.

In adolescence, they showed up as:

    overthinking every reaction from others,

    fear of disappointing people,

    trying to be perfect,

    avoiding conflict at all costs.

In early relationships, they showed up as:

    staying quiet when something hurt me,

    accepting behavior I didn't want,

    believing it was safer to comply than express discomfort,

    choosing peace over honesty.

In adulthood, they showed up as:

    anxiety when someone raised their voice,

shutting down during emotional conversations,

tolerating mistreatment at work,

performing competence while hiding exhaustion,

feeling responsible for everyone's emotions but my own.

Triggers aren't random.

They're survival patterns, repeating themselves.

It builds structures inside you, rooms full of feelings you never unpacked, closets full of memories you pushed behind you, floors laid over moments you didn't want to look at.

And emotional triggers are the cracks in that structure; the places where the old emotions try to push through.

Triggers don't come from weakness.

They come from survival.

They are the leftover pieces of a childhood spent absorbing more than any child should.

The more I stayed silent, the more I disappeared.

Not all at once.

But slowly.

Incrementally.

A swallowed feeling here.

A forced smile there.

A boundary unspoken.

A truth buried.

A need denied.   42

Until one day, I didn't know what I liked, disliked, wanted, or feared,
    only what would keep the peace.

Part 1 Summary

I survived childhood through silence. Silence forms the storm.

It holds everything in, swirling, building pressure year after year.

This part of my life didn't make me the storm.

It prepared me for it.

But one day, the storm would break open;

And, so would I.

Because later, when the world brought more chaos, more abandonment, more harm, more upheaval…

I would discover that I wasn't just surviving storms,

I was becoming one.

Part 2: Stirring the Storm

Some storms arrive as weather.

Others arrive as people.

You don't have to be struck by lightning to be electrified by fear.
Sometimes, the most dangerous storms are the ones that sound like love.

Section 1: Love

Winds

The first gust of a storm is never the strongest, but it's the one you remember.

It's the breath before the breaking.

The shift in the air tells you something is coming.

Some winds don't clear the sky.

They just stir up everything you thought was settled.

Love was that wind.

It felt like a possibility.

It sounded like a promise.

It moved through me like weather I couldn't yet name.

Chapter 8: First Love, First Lessons

There is something sacred about a girl's first love.

Not because of what happens on the outside,

    but because of what it awakens on the inside.

First love is the mirror showing you who you think you are,

    and who you fear you will never be.

I was fourteen when I first felt the flutter of being chosen.

Not chosen out of responsibility or convenience,

    but chosen because someone genuinely liked me.

His name was Dan.

He was funny, bold, and a little rebellious in a way that felt exciting rather than dangerous. He talked openly, laughed loudly, and carried himself with a confidence I didn't understand. He saw me in a way I wasn't used to being seen: curious, attentive, wanting to be near me.

For a girl who had spent her childhood shrinking herself, that kind of attention felt like sunlight.

I didn't know how to receive it, but I wanted it.

I didn't know how to trust it, but I leaned toward it.

And I didn't know how to protect myself, because I had never been taught how.

When you've been raised in silence, validation feels like oxygen.

I had spent years being told to quiet myself, to minimize myself, to carry my feelings alone. So, when someone finally looked at me with admiration instead of expectation, it lit up a part of me I didn't even know was dark.

This is the danger of entering adolescence without boundaries.

Affection feels like obligation.

Attention feels like debt.

Being wanted feels like being responsible for someone else's happiness.

I didn't know how to say no.

I didn't know how to express discomfort.

I didn't know it was okay to be unsure.

I didn't know my feelings mattered.

So much of my early relationship with Dan wasn't about desire,

    it was about wanting to be accepted.

And wanting to be accepted when you've grown up feeling unimportant is a powerful force.

It makes you override your instincts.

It makes you stay quiet when you're confused.

It makes you pretend you're fine even when you're not.

I didn't understand any of this then.

I only knew I didn't want to lose him.

The world had taught me love required compliance.

My entire childhood was a study in compliance.

Don't upset adults.

Don't draw attention.

Don't express emotions.

Don't make demands.

Don't be difficult.

Don't be inconvenient.

When sex is normalized to not be special, then you think it is normal. It is what you are "supposed to do". So, I fell back on what I knew.

Stay quiet.

Go along.

Don't cause a problem.

Don't risk losing someone.

Girls who grow up afraid to speak rarely learn how to, or that they should, advocate for themselves in their early relationships.

And I was one of those girls.

It's strange how early patterns repeat themselves.

I had already learned to hide my true feelings around adults.

Now I was learning to hide them around boys.

I didn't want to disappoint anyone.

I didn't want to seem childish.

I didn't want to risk rejection.

I didn't want to be "too emotional."

So, I went along.

I confused the attention with being special.

I confused teenage hormones with a man's love.

Silence in childhood had trained me well.

When you grow up minimizing your own feelings,

你 you enter adolescence already primed to minimize your boundaries.

I will never forget the moment a teacher quietly pulled me aside and said:

"He's… more advanced than you. Be careful."

I didn't understand what she meant.

I didn't know how to interpret warnings from adults.

I didn't know how to say, 'What does that mean?' 'What should I look out for?'

So, I laughed it off - with him.

I didn't realize she was trying to protect me.

I didn't realize she saw something I didn't.

I didn't realize adults could step in with guidance, because they never had before.

In my young teens, I thought:

    love was supposed to be confusing,

    love was supposed to feel scary,

    love was supposed to involve pressure,

    love was supposed to require self-silencing,

    love was supposed to hurt sometimes.

Because that was the only model I had.

No one taught me love should feel safe.

No one taught me love should include boundaries.

No one taught me I had a right to my own comfort.

No one taught me difference between affection and obligation.

So, I followed the script I had learned at home.

Don't question.

Don't speak.

Don't make anyone upset.

Don't take up space.

First love should be a gentle introduction to intimacy.

Mine was a crash course in losing myself.

He wasn't a villain.

He wasn't dangerous.

He wasn't even irresponsible for his age.

He was simply the first boy to reflect back the patterns my childhood had already carved into me.

The story of this isn't about what happened between us;

it's about what it meant.

A young girl who didn't know her worth.

A young girl who didn't know she had a voice.

A young girl who mistook attention for love.

A young girl who didn't yet understand what she deserved.

A young girl who believed affection had to be earned through compliance.

This isn't about Dan.

It's about me.

It's the beginning of the storm brewing inside a girl who had been taught her entire life to stay small.

First love taught me something I didn't realize back then.

You cannot build a relationship on silence, and expect to feel seen.

Chapter 9: Lover, Protector, Womanizer

Mike was perfect.

Intellectual, funny, adventurous.

He entered my world at a time when I was still learning how to be a person, not just a survivor, not just a daughter, not just a girl following rules, but a thinking, feeling, curious human being.

With Mike, I felt alive.

He didn't just talk *to* me; he talked *with* me.

We stayed up all night discussing philosophy, science, art, politics, dreams.

He introduced me to books I'd never heard of, music I'd never felt, ideas that stretched my understanding of what was possible.

He saw intelligence in me and reflected it back—not as a novelty, but as a fact.

For the first time, I felt smart.

Not just "smart for a girl."

Smart, period.

He also taught me how to fight back.

Not with fists, but with words.

With presence.

With refusal.

Mike was my shield before I learned to be my own.

He modeled a kind of courage I hadn't known was possible: the courage to say *This is not okay* without apology.

But Mike was also a womanizer.

And that word feels too small for what he was.

He wasn't cruel about it.

He wasn't deceptive.

At least, that's what I told myself, until the day I learned the difference between discreet and dishonest.

It wasn't a gradual fade.

It wasn't a slow drift apart.

It was a door left slightly ajar.

A silence in the house that felt too thick, too still.

I pushed the bedroom door open.

And there he was.

In bed.

With her.

Time didn't slow down.

It shattered.

My vision blurred at the edges, sharpening only on the details I didn't want to see.

The surprise in his eyes, not guilt, not shame, but annoyance, as if I'd interrupted something minor.

The way she hid from me, scared to face me.

My stomach dropped.

My lungs emptied.

The floor beneath me didn't feel like wood anymore; it felt like nothing.

I was falling through the center of my own life.

I didn't scream.

I didn't cry.

I just stood there, frozen in the doorway, while my heart pounded so hard I thought it would crack my ribs.

Betrayal isn't always loud.

Sometimes it's the quietest thing in the room,

    a silence so complete it drowns out everything else.

He said my name.

Once.

Like a question.

Like I was the one who didn't belong.

Other women were more important to him than I was.

And in that moment, I wasn't even a woman, I was an inconvenience.

A disruption to his pleasure.

A problem to be managed later.

It took me years to understand that Mike didn't betray me because I wasn't enough.

He betrayed me because he was never truly mine to lose.

What he gave me was real.

He showed me I could think outside the box.

He showed me I was smart.

He showed me I deserved to be defended.

But what he took from me was real, too.

The belief that intimacy meant safety.

The trust that someone who praised my mind would honor my heart.

The illusion that love could be both thrilling and true.

Mike was my guiding light until he became the dark.

And when his light went out, it didn't fade—

it was blown out, suddenly, brutally, like the lightning in the storm

.

Chapter 10: Entertain Me but Don't Love Me

When I first saw Christopher, my heart stopped.

My stomach erupted into a million butterflies in flight.

He walked with an air of confidence bordering on arrogance, the kind that feels magnetic rather than threatening.

He moved through rooms as if he owned them, and for a while, he made me feel like I owned them, too.

We didn't start off dating.

We eased into it, conversations that stretched into nights, glances that held a second too long, a slow, delicious tension that felt like a game we were both playing.

I was a young adult, just out of college, starting a new life.

He was accomplished, cocky, and could make any woman feel like she was the only one in the room.

He was also clear from the beginning:

We will never be serious.

We will not fall in love.

I will never marry you.

He said it with a smile, as if he were doing me a favor,

giving me the rules so I wouldn't get hurt.

And I believed him.

I believed him so completely that I never stopped to listen for the change in his heart.

I never noticed when his voice softened, when his rules began to bend, when his *never* quietly became *maybe*.

Maybe with you.

But I didn't know.

He never told me.

He never said, *I was wrong.*

He never said, *My feelings have changed.*

He never said, *You're not temporary to me anymore.*

So I lived inside the story he had written for us:

a beautiful, finite story.

A fling.

An adventure.

A temporary arrangement.

And because I believed I was only temporary, I started looking for someone who would want me permanently.

Not out of malice.

Not out of revenge.

Out of fear.

Out of that old, familiar ache that whispered:

You are not worthy enough to stay.

Then …he knew what I had done.

And in that moment, the world tipped sideways.

We tried to talk through it, to rebuild what my carelessness had broken.

But trust isn't a thing you can reassemble with apologies.

It's a mirror. Once cracked, you can still see yourself in it, but the reflection is forever split.

And Christopher and I were left staring at each other through the fractures.

I had done to him exactly what others had done to me.

I had assumed.

I had doubted.

I had hidden my truth while resenting him for seeing me as a "liability".

I had made him pay for the sins of people who weren't him.

I had become the kind of person I thought I was protecting myself from.

And I hated it.

I hated myself for it.

But hating myself didn't change what I had done.

It didn't undo the lie, the doubt, the assumption that he could never really want me.

It didn't give us back what we had before.

We held on for a little while, tense conversations, careful touches, days that felt like walking through a house after a storm;

everything still standing, but nothing feeling safe.

We were two people trying to rebuild on a foundation I had shattered.

And some foundations can't be repaired.

Some trust can't be relearned.

So, we let go.

Not with a fight, not with drama, but with a quiet, mutual exhaustion.

We parted as gently as two people can when they're both bleeding from the same wound.

He moved away.

I stayed.

The space between us became literal, then permanent.

I lost him.

Not because he didn't love me.

Not because I didn't love him.

But because I hadn't believed him capable of loving me,

and in my disbelief, I made it true.

Christopher taught me that you can break someone's heart without meaning to.

That you can become the storm in someone else's life even when you're still learning to navigate your own.

That sometimes the person you're running from is yourself, and you don't realize it until you've already run someone else over.

I lost the man I loved because I was too busy protecting myself from a loss that hadn't happened yet.

And in the end, I became the cause of my own fear.

Chapter 11: Love as Control

Some relationships arrive like a lightning bolt:

bright, electric, impossible to ignore.

Hector was that bolt.

He was charismatic, magnetic, funny, and sharp.

He made me laugh in a way I hadn't laughed in a long time.

He saw me with a kind of intensity that felt flattering, intoxicating even.

He made me feel alive.

That matters after years of carrying the weight of motherhood alone.

That matters after years of being responsible for everything and everyone.

That matters when you've been ignored or diminished by partners before him.

Hector was a spark.

A flame.

A burst of something exciting and new.

But the thing about fire is this:

you don't always notice when it starts to burn you.

The early days were perfect, maybe too perfect.

At first, we were inseparable.

We had inside jokes.

We talked nonstop.

We explored, laughed, and shared dreams.

It felt like I finally met someone who matched my energy,

    someone who didn't need me to carry him,

    someone who wasn't passive or absent,

    someone who saw me as extraordinary.

He made me believe in possibility.

And after everything I had gone through,

    I wanted possibility.

But early intensity can hide early warning signs.

His attention was consuming.

His affection was overwhelming.

His interest was constant.

And I mistook that intensity for love;

    something many women mistake when they've been starved for genuine connection.

The shift was subtle at first.

Tiny comments.

Little questions.

Moments I shrugged off because I wanted to see the best in him.

"Who were you talking to?"

"Why did you smile at that?"

"Why did he look at you like that?"

"You didn't tell me about this."

At first, it felt like curiosity.

Then it felt like surveillance.

Jealousy became a language he spoke fluently.

At first, it was a joke.

Then a comment.

Then an argument.

Then a pattern.

If a man passed by shirtless at the beach,

    something completely normal, it was a problem.

If I mentioned running into a coworker,

    even an innocent interaction, it sparked suspicion.

If a movie featured an actor I thought was attractive

    (even casually, even years earlier),

    it became an interrogation.

My world began to shrink.

The space between what was allowed and what would set him off
grew thin.

Living with unpredictability was nothing new to me.

I had survived it my entire childhood.

But now it was wrapped in the voice of someone I loved.

Control doesn't always look like control at first.

Control isn't loud; it is pressure.

Hector isolated me slowly:

questioning me about my friends,

questioning me about my coworkers,

questioning me about my family,

questioning me about my choices,

questioning me about my motives,

questioning me about my emotions,

If he didn't approve of someone,

he made it known.

Over time, I saw less and less of the people who kept me grounded.

He didn't have to forbid anything;

he simply made it uncomfortable to choose anything but him.

That's how unhealthy relationships take over:

by making your life smaller

until they are the center of the shrinking universe.

The loneliness that comes from being controlled is deep.

At first, it felt right.

So, he moved in.

He became part of the household.

He intertwined himself into my daily life.

But instead of feeling united,

I felt suffocated.

Instead of feeling supported,

I felt monitored.

Instead of feeling safe,

I felt watched.

My home, my sanctuary, the space I worked so hard to build for my children, became tense, unpredictable, thick with anxiety.

My daughters stayed upstairs away from him, but that also meant me.

My son pushed back, bold in his own way, to push his buttons and escalate the situation, but it only heightened the tension.

Home stopped feeling like home.

And isolation became a new form of silence.

As time went on, the arguments changed.

They weren't about little things anymore.

They were about my beliefs,

    or more accurately,

    the beliefs he demanded I adopt.

He was deeply political.

Deeply reactive.

Deeply entrenched in a worldview that left no room for nuance.

I wasn't political,

    not in the way he wanted me to be.

I didn't believe leadership defined everything.

I didn't tie my identity to parties or politicians.

I believed life was bigger, deeper, more complex.

But to him, disagreement wasn't just conflict;

    it was betrayal.

Even neutrality upset him.

He wanted alignment, not autonomy.

Submission, not dialogue.

And suddenly the arguments weren't about other people;

they were about me.

There wasn't one moment.

There were hundreds:

The days he was so angry he sat in the middle of the house blasting the TV so loudly the neighbors could hear.

The days my daughters were afraid to come downstairs.

The days my son argued with him and the air turned dangerous with tension.

The days he accused me of irrationality for asking his son not to jump on furniture, I worked myself to exhaustion to afford.

The days I realized my body was tight before he even came home.

The days I felt myself disappear just to avoid another fight.

Then the day I realized that if I didn't leave,

my children would learn this as love.

That was the final straw.

I couldn't let them grow up believing that love meant control,

    that attention meant possession,

    that pressure meant passion,

    that intensity meant care.

No.

This ended with me.

So, I told him to leave.

He moved out.

But the relationship lingered for years, six long years,

    because leaving someone's home is easier than leaving their pull.

His grip loosened slowly, painfully.

One boundary at a time.

One awakening at a time.

But eventually,

    the storm inside me grew louder than his voice.

I chose myself.

This isn't about harshness, it's about clarity.

Hector wasn't a monster.

He was a man shaped by his own wounds,

    his own jealousy,

    his own insecurities,

    his own desire for control.

But understanding someone's wounds does not require you to live inside them.

Walking away wasn't an act of anger.

It was an act of survival.

It wasn't about rejecting him.

It was about reclaiming me.

The storm inside me wasn't chaotic anymore.

It was directional.

Purposeful.

Focused.

This was the moment I transitioned from:

suppressed to aware,

controlled to conscious,

reactive to intentional,

silent to self-defined.

I wasn't just surviving relationships anymore.

I was learning to examine them.

To question what was offered.

To evaluate what was demanded.

To measure what was being taken from me versus what was being given.

And for the first time in my life, I chose freedom —

over fear,

over pressure,

over control,

over belonging.

I stopped confusing intensity for love.

I stopped mistaking passion for partnership.

I realized love should never require you to abandon yourself.

Love that diminishes you is not love.

Love that isolates you is not love.

Love that controls you is not love.

And love that fears your strength will always try to suppress your storm.

Section 2: Marriage

The Sky Darkens

Storms don't rush.

They gather.

They build in layers, a drop in pressure, a thickening of clouds, a heaviness in the air you learn to wear like skin.

These storms are not about a single lightning strike.

It's about the long, low rumble of a sky that never quite clears.

Chapter 12: Carrying the Weight

There are moments in life when you don't realize you're becoming the backbone of an entire household until the weight becomes impossible to ignore.

Motherhood didn't just make me stronger.

It revealed a strength that had been growing quietly inside me since childhood.

When I was young, I survived instability.

In adolescence, I survived emotional chaos.

But in adulthood, I survived something different:

> being responsible for everything
>
> while being supported by no one.

He entered my life softly, and stayed soft

His name is Israel.

Israel wasn't dramatic or unpredictable.

He wasn't cruel.

He wasn't volatile.

He was calm, easygoing, steady, qualities I had always craved.

For a girl who grew up reading rooms for danger, his steadiness felt like safety.

He was the first person who didn't bring emotional storms into my home.

But I didn't yet understand that safety isn't just the absence of conflict, it's the presence of accountability.

Israel wanted a future, a family, a home;

but he didn't know how to carry the weight of those dreams.

I remember standing outside on my birthday, looking up at the sky,

and saying the most honest prayer I had ever spoken:

"If I could just have a baby boy…it would be the greatest gift of my life."

Two weeks later, I was pregnant.

I felt chosen.

Seen.

Blessed.

Finally allowed something good.

From the moment I knew I was carrying him,

I loved him with a ferocity that startled me.

Andres became the center of my universe.

Every dream, every plan, every decision, all of it revolved around giving him the life I never had.

But love wasn't the only thing shaping my pregnancy.

Responsibility was.

Israel didn't have a job when I became pregnant.

He wasn't contributing financially.

He wasn't building the foundation we needed.

But I told myself it was temporary.

That he would figure it out.

That he would step up when it mattered.

So, I worked.

And worked.

And worked.

Long hours, stressful projects, and business travel, all of which broke my heart every time I had to leave Andres once he arrived.

I told myself I could handle it;

    because I always had.

But when the person you love doesn't carry their share of the load,

You slowly become both parents at once:

    the provider,

    the nurturer,

    the protector,

    the planner,

the decision-maker,

the emotional anchor,

the everything.

Israel stayed home with Andres, but staying home is not the same as showing up.

He was present, but he wasn't involved.

Not in the way a child needs.

Not in the way a partner should be.

We bought a house,

because I saved, I planned, I sacrificed.

We upgraded to a bigger house,

because I worked, I strategized, and I held the finances together.

I traveled for work,

because someone had to bring in money.

I stayed up late to finish projects,

because I was terrified of failing my family.

And still, Israel didn't look for work.

I remember coming home one night at midnight after a long day, exhausted, emotionally drained, desperate to sleep.

He asked me to stop and get milk for Andrew.

Milk.

He had been home all day.

And something inside me broke.

It wasn't about milk.

It was about everything:

    the imbalance,

    the dependency,

    the lack of effort,

    the absence of partnership,

    the betrayal of trust,

    the exhaustion of carrying a family alone.

I wasn't just tired.

I was done.

I told him the truth,

    the truth I had swallowed for too long.

I didn't believe him anymore,

I didn't feel supported,

I had lost respect for him,

I couldn't continue building a life with someone who refused to build anything in return.

It hurt.

It hurt him.

It hurt me.

But honesty is sometimes the kindest thing you can give yourself.

He said he would change.

He said he would try.

He said he would get a job.

But after years of promises that never materialized,

    I couldn't believe him. I didn't respect him.

He left.

He moved out of the country.

And from that moment on,

    he was gone.

Andrew lost his father.

And I became a single mother,

    with no safety net,

    no co-parent,

    no break,

    and no alternative but to rise.

Long before Israel left, I had been carrying the emotional and financial weight alone.

The only difference now was honesty.

I learned something important through that chapter of my life:

There is nothing more powerful than a woman who realizes she can do it by herself,

because she already has.

Motherhood didn't break me.

It forged me.

It taught me endurance, intuition, resilience, compassion, and fire.

It taught me to build the kind of life for my son no one had built for me.

He didn't know it then,

But he saved me.

He gave me purpose.

He gave me direction.

He gave me clarity.

He gave me motivation.

He gave me the love I had longed for my entire life.

Raising him alone didn't feel like a burden.

It felt like redemption.

I wasn't repeating my childhood.

I was rewriting it.

Every sacrifice was worth it.

Every late night.

Every long workday.

Every tear.

Every moment of exhaustion.

He was the proof that I could create something good out of a life that had given me so much chaos.

Chapter 13: When Pressure Masquerades as Love

Some relationships don't break you all at once.

They break you by degrees.

Not through violence, not through rage, not through chaos,

but through subtle erosion:

> your boundaries,

> your confidence,

> your intuition,

> your sense of self.

And sometimes the most dangerous kind of harm is the kind wrapped in logic, calmness, or what looks like understanding.

That was my relationship with Ron.

It began simply enough.

He was stable.

Practical.

Predictable.

A man who gave the impression of structure, and after the instability of my past relationships, that felt comforting.

It was a new relationship looking like a shiny star.

He was a father.

He worked.

He had a routine.

He knew how to talk about logistics and life plans.

He seemed like the responsible choice.

But responsible is not the same as respectful.

And predictable is not the same as safe.

When your voice has been conditioned into silence, coercion sounds like reason.

The moment that changed everything started as a conversation.

Nothing dramatic.

Nothing loud.

Nothing that would raise red flags to an outsider.

He asked me to do something I did not want to do,

    something involving bringing another person into our intimacy.

He framed it as excitement.

As exploration.

As something "fun."

As something he had done before with someone else.

As something that would keep us "connected."

I didn't want to.

Every part of my body said no.

My intuition screamed.

My discomfort was real and immediate.

But here is the truth about women who weren't taught to protect themselves:

> We override our instincts before we question other people's expectations.

So instead of saying no,

I convinced myself I was overreacting.

Maybe this was normal.

Maybe this was what good partners did.

That maybe I needed to be more open, more flexible, more accommodating.

Accommodation had been the defining theme of my life.

And it followed me here too.

He wasn't yelling.

He wasn't threatening.

He wasn't angry.

He was simply insisting, persistently, steadily, confidently, until my resistance felt like the problem.

Coercion doesn't always sound like force.

Sometimes it sounds like persuasion.

Or compromise.

Or, worst of all:

"If you love me…"

So, I reached out to someone from my past,

someone I cared for deeply,

someone I had unfinished feelings for,

someone who represented emotional truth in a way no one ever had.

That part of the story was mine.

My choice.

My heart.

But the reason I did it was not.

I did it because I felt obligated.

I did it because I didn't want to lose the stability I thought I was being offered.

I did it because I had been conditioned to prioritize someone else's wants over my own wellbeing.

And that moment, that decision, it was the deepest act of self-abandonment I had ever made.

It awakened something in me.

Something painful.

Something powerful.

Because the moment you betray yourself,

You finally see the truth of your situation:

This new man didn't want a *Partner*.

He wanted control.

The clearest evidence of this came later, in a moment that still stings:

He went through my phone.

Found the number of the person I had reached out to.

Called him without telling me.

Told him everything,

    he turned it all on me,

He made me look perverted, disgusting

He weaponized the lie, the story.

He exposed me to someone else in an attempt to shame me into compliance.

To frighten me into choosing him.

To control an outcome that should have belonged to me alone.

Even after all the signs,

  all the instincts,

  all the warnings…

I craved stability, so I pushed down my own worries,

I married him.

He stood beside me in dress clothes.

I stood there pregnant with twins,

feeling the pressure of expectation, obligation, investment, and timing.

My stepfather looked at me and saw the truth in my eyes.

He said:

  "We can leave right now. You don't have to do this."

If he could see it, it must have been written all over me.

But I felt trapped. Trapped by:

  responsibility,

  finances,

  expectations,

  the belief that I had to finish what I started,

  the idea that having children meant I had to stay.

So, I said "I do."

Not because I wanted to,

　　but because I didn't see another path.

I abandoned myself again that day.

And the cost was high.

Marriage didn't change him, it revealed him

The financial burden landed squarely on me.

Again.

The responsibility landed on me.

Again.

The emotional load landed on me.

Again.

He quit his job shortly after we married,

　　a job that paid well,

　　a job that supported his other children,

　　a job that represented stability.

He replaced it with something entry-level.

Something that drained resources.

It shifted everything onto my shoulders.

And when we had our twins, my beautiful daughters,

　　my world both expanded and collapsed.

I was caring for newborns,

    two boys,

    a household,

    a marriage,

    a full-time job,

    and a man who kept choosing escape over partnership.

I worked until the day I delivered.

I picked up the children, came home exhausted, and carried the family
alone while he slept during the day,

    went to the gym when he woke,

    worked nights,

    and remained emotionally unavailable.

This time, I wasn't just disappearing for a partner.

I was disappearing for an entire life.

Every request feels reasonable until you add them together.

Then you realize you've become the engine powering the entire
relationship.

Not because he couldn't do things,

    but because he refused to.

Coercion taught me a hard truth.

Some men don't want an equal, they want a source:

   a source of labor,

   a source of support,

   a source of stability,

   a source of energy,

   a source of love,

   but not a partner.

The ending wasn't loud, it was inevitable.

It took the betrayal with another woman, though there were many women. It was a marriage filled with:

   the lies,

   the secrecy,

   the hidden phone,

   the absence…

   to give me the final push.

He wanted freedom.

He took it.

But what he didn't realize was this:

   His leaving freed me too.

I reclaimed my life.

I reclaimed my stability.

I reclaimed my voice.

I reclaimed my sense of self.

Leaving didn't break me.

Staying would have.

This chapter isn't about him.

It's about awakening.

Awakening to the truth that consent is more than yes or no.

Awakening to the reality that "support" without effort is exploitation.

Awakening to the fact that coercion can sound calm, polite, patient, or loving, *but it is still coercion.*

Awakening to the understanding that your body knows the truth before your mind does.

Awakening to the strength required to walk away from a life you built, even when it's the only life you've known.

This is the chapter where I stopped mistaking responsibility for love.

Where I stopped confusing obligation with devotion.

Where I stopped abandoning myself to preserve someone else's comfort.

Where I learned the most powerful truth of my adulthood:

Love that requires you to shrink is not love.

It is captivity.

And I was not born to be contained.

I was born to become the storm, and I was now aware of it.

Section 3: Lessons Learned

The Quiet Before the Voice

Some storms don't rage in the sky,

    they build beneath the skin.

In the silence that becomes its own kind of thunder.

This is the quiet before the storm.

The pressure, gathering inside me like a charge waiting for ground.

The storm is not the weather outside,

    but the climate within.

The storm was no longer outside me.

It was my own, inside, rising.

Chapter 14: How to Say No (When You Were Never Taught)

There is a moment in every girl's life when she realizes the world expects her to manage other people's comfort more than her own.

Some girls learn this slowly.

I learned it young.

By the time I reached adolescence, I had already mastered the art of being agreeable.

Of accommodating.

Of anticipating.

Of shrinking.

Not because I wanted to be that way,

    but because I had been trained to survive that way.

When a girl grows up without emotional protection, boundaries, or adults who explain her rights or guide her through the complexities of adolescence, she enters adolescence unprepared.

Not unprepared academically.

Not unprepared socially.

Unprepared emotionally.

Unprepared to protect herself.

Unprepared to use her voice.

Unprepared to recognize discomfort.

Unprepared to set boundaries.

Unprepared to say no.

The world taught me what compliance looked like, never consent.

Consent was not a concept in my childhood home.

Not with emotions.

Not with responsibilities.

Not with expectations.

I was taught:

    to submit to adult moods,

    to do what was asked without question,

    to put adult needs before my own,

    to avoid conflict by going along,

    to endure rather than object.

These lessons seep into a girl's wiring.

So by the time she is twelve, thirteen, fourteen, she doesn't just avoid saying no;

    she doesn't believe she's allowed to.

That was me.

I didn't know I had permission to choose.

I didn't know I had permission to pause.

I didn't know I had permission to feel unsure.

I didn't know I had permission to protect myself.

No one tells you silence in childhood creates confusion in adolescence, confusion about your instincts,

about your worth,

about your right to take up space in your own story.

My early adolescence was full of moments where I felt a flicker of discomfort but didn't know what to do with it. I didn't have the tools to name it, let alone honor it.

So instead of listening to the quiet warning inside me, I drowned it out with compliance.

If someone liked me, I felt I had to like them back.

If someone wanted something from me, I felt responsible for giving it.

If someone pushed past my hesitation, I assumed they knew better.

If I felt confused, I chose silence rather than risk conflict.

If I feared rejection, I convinced myself I was overreacting.

I didn't know how to tell the difference

between pressure and affection,

between interest and expectation,

between wanting something and tolerating it.

No one had ever taught me to check in with myself.

And when you don't know yourself, it's easy for others to write your story for you.

Looking back now, I can see moments when my body tried to speak for me:

the tightness in my chest,

the pit in my stomach,

the hesitation in my voice,

the urge to pull away,

the instinct to freeze.

These were signs.

Signals.

Warnings.

But when you grow up being told to ignore your feelings,

you learn to ignore your body too.

Instinct becomes something you silence.

Discomfort becomes something you rationalize.

Fear becomes something you swallow.

Boundaries become something you never develop.

My body tried to tell me the truth, but my mind had been trained to dismiss anything that didn't make other people comfortable.

There is a loneliness in not knowing how to protect yourself.

Middle school and early high school are confusing enough for kids who have guidance.

But for girls like me, girls who grew up without emotional anchors, it is a minefield.

I watched other girls say no easily, casually.

I watched them refuse things without guilt.

I watched them walk away from situations that made them uncomfortable.

I watched them express opinions without fear.

I didn't understand how they did it.

The courage it took for them to set a boundary was foreign to me.

It felt like watching someone speak a language I wasn't taught.

So, I stayed silent.

Not because I wanted to, but because I didn't have an alternative.

When no one teaches you to say no, you learn to live your life in "yes," even when your heart is saying something else.

When silence becomes your default response, your boundaries become porous.

Your worth becomes negotiable.

Your instincts become quiet.

Your discomfort becomes expected.

Your voice becomes something you only use to keep the peace.

I wasn't choosing my life,

    I was reacting to it.

I didn't know how to question.

I didn't know how to advocate.

I didn't know how to push back.

I didn't know how to trust my own uncertainty.

And because I didn't know how to say no,

I said yes to people, to situations, to expectations a girl who had been taught her worth would have walked away from instantly.

That is the cost of a childhood without emotional protection.

Not the moment you lose your voice,

    but the moment you realize

    you never learned how to use it.

But this chapter is not about blame, it's about realization.

It happens in small realizations.

The awareness your discomfort matters.

The understanding you deserved more guidance.

The recognition you weren't protected the way you should have been.

The clarity of saying no is not rebellion; it's self-respect.

The shift from compliance to consciousness.

It is when the storm inside me whispered,

You deserve to choose.

You deserve to speak.

You deserve to feel safe.

You deserve to say no.

This is where survival begins to transform into identity,

where the girl who was never taught to use her voice

begins to imagine she might actually have one.

Part 2: Summary

This isn't about heartbreak.

It is the beginning of questioning.

The beginning of noticing the cracks.

The beginning of waking up.

It's about awakening:

awakening to your worth,

awakening to your capability,

awakening to your strength,

awakening to your power.

This is where the girl who survived storms,

became the woman who could withstand hurricanes.

A woman who could rebuild life from nothing.

A woman who could protect her children fiercely.

A woman who could carry four lives on her shoulders and not crumble.

A woman who could stand alone,

and stand tall.

It is the beginning of my transformation.

Part 3 : Awakening the Storm

There comes a moment in every storm when the sky cracks open.

When what was hidden becomes visible.

When what was silent becomes a roar.

This is when lightning strikes—not once, but again and again.

The weather turns harsh.

Some storms don't just pass through you—

they change the very ground you stand on.

It is not about surviving the rain.

It's about surviving the strike.

Chapter 15: The Door That Closed

Some moments don't just disappoint you,

> they change the trajectory of your life.

This is one of those turning points.

It's the moment where your talent, your brilliance, your passion, and your potential come face-to-face with something bigger than you,

> the limits of the adults in your world.

Because dreams don't die on their own.

They get shut down,

> sometimes by the very people who were supposed to nurture them.

I wasn't just smart, I was driven.

School wasn't an escape for me.

It was a purpose.

Where home felt unpredictable, school felt structured.

Where adults were unstable, teachers were steady.

Where emotions were unwelcome, intellect was rewarded.

Where silence was expected, achievement spoke for me.

I excelled, not because it was easy,

but because it was the one place where my effort matched my outcome.

Then I found something even more powerful, a field that spoke to the deepest part of me:

psychoneuroimmunology.

The study of how the mind can heal the body.

How thoughts can change physiology.

How trauma and stress shape health.

How the brain and immune system speak to each other.

It was as if someone had handed me a map of my own life.

Finally, something made sense:

Healing wasn't abstract.

It was biological.

It was real.

It was possible.

It was measurable.

I didn't just want to study it,

  I wanted to devote my life to it.

And a professor saw that in me.

For the first time, an adult recognized my brilliance without diminishing it or turning away from it.

He told me something no one else had ever said so plainly:

"You can go farther than this. You can go all the way."

My professor prepared research with me.

Co-wrote papers with me.

Pushed me academically.

Believed in me.

And then came the opportunity.

I could enter a PhD program immediately, no master's required.

A fast track.

A recognition of excellence.

A door that rarely opens for anyone.

It was everything I had worked for,

    everything I wanted,

    everything I dreamed of…

    …and everything I was talked out of.

Not by professors.

Not by advisors.

By my own family.

Dreams are easy to crush when the dreamer is used to being silenced.

I was tired.

Tired from working three jobs just to afford school.

Tired from being responsible for myself since childhood.

Tired from carrying adult burdens before I even had a chance to be one.

And instead of support,

    instead of encouragement,

    instead of help navigating financial aid,

    instead of someone saying, "We'll figure this out,"

I heard other reasons.

"That degree won't make you any money."

"You need to get a job."

"You need to start your life."

"You can't afford to keep going."

"That field is nonsense."

"Stop dreaming."

There is nothing heavier than trying to carry a dream in a family that doesn't believe in dreams.

My education was supposed to be the path out of the chaos I grew up in.

A new life.

A new environment.

A new identity not defined by survival.

And for a moment, I saw the door.

Open.

Wide.

Inviting.

But every time I reached for it, someone else pushed it closed.

I didn't know what financial aid could do for me.

No one guided me.

No one explained scholarships.

No one walked me through the process.

I was exhausted,

unsupported,

and emotionally depleted.

So instead of choosing my dream,

I chose what had always been chosen for me.

Survival.

I said no to the PhD.

Not because I wanted to.

Because I didn't see another option.

It wasn't dramatic.

There were no tears.

No big conversation.

No celebration.

No mourning.

Just a quiet, heartbreaking surrender.

I took a job.

A regular job.

A job that paid the bills.

A job that felt like settling because it was.

A job that pushed my dreams into the background and forced me into the practical version of adulthood, my family preferred.

And in that moment, another part of me went silent.

Not the child this time, but the future version of me that wanted more.

People talk about doors closing as if they're always tragic.

But sometimes the closing of that one meaningful door awakens another part of you,

    the part that decides.

I will not let others define my limits.

I will not let my dreams be dismissed.

I will not let my worth be determined by people who can't see it.

That was the moment I understood something profound.

My life was never going to be shaped by the opportunities given to me.

It was going to be shaped by the opportunities I created, demanded, or reclaimed.

Even though I didn't pursue the PhD, it never stopped calling to me:

in the work I chose,

in the way I thought,

in the way I mothered,

in the way I healed.

The dream didn't die.

It simply waited.

And one day, after surviving all the storms life had yet to throw at me, I would come back to it, not as a lost student,

but as a woman who knew her worth.

This is where I realized one simple truth:

When someone shuts a door on you, learn to build a new one.

And I did.

Again.

And again.

But what came next would test me even more.

Chapter 16: A Betrayal in Writing

I didn't expect betrayal to come from a woman of my same age.

Men had dismissed me.

Men had underestimated me.

Men had talked over me.

Men had taken credit for my work.

That was the architecture of working in a male-dominated industry.

But I never expected the deepest cut to come from someone I believed would understand me,

    a woman navigating the same world I was trying to survive in.

She looked like an ally, until she wasn't.

When I first started working under her, I thought we were building something real.

A mutual respect.

A sense of solidarity.

She praised my work in meetings.

She smiled in hallways.

She asked about my kids.

She positioned herself as a supporter.

I believed her.

Every word.

Every compliment.

Every gesture of camaraderie.

Because women don't get many allies in these environments.

We take what we can get.

We cling to it.

We hope it means something.

But some people know how to weaponize hope.

She gave me my annual review verbally,

    warm, encouraging, and full of supportive feedback.

She said she hadn't filled out the written document yet, but everything she was saying reflected what she would write.

I trusted her.

She was a woman.

A leader.

Someone I thought was building me up.

Months later, I opened the written review.

What I saw felt like a punch to the chest.

It was harsh.

Cold.

Unrecognizable.

A contradiction of everything she had said aloud.

It wasn't constructive.

It wasn't honest.

It wasn't aligned.

It was sabotage.

The words on that page cut deeper than any performance issue ever could, because they revealed something far worse.

She never saw me as an ally.

She saw me as competition.

I went to her boss, shaking,

    not from anger,

    but from heartbreak.

I wanted someone to witness the betrayal.

To see how wrong it was.

To see how cruel it felt to be misled by someone who pretended to support me.

I expected confusion.

Concern.

Maybe an apology on her behalf.

Instead, I heard hedging.

Excuses.

Defensiveness.

The system was protecting itself,

    and she was part of that system.

That's when the truth landed.

Some women in male-dominated industries don't lift other women up because they're too afraid of losing their own footing.

They learn to survive by aligning with the men in power,

    not the women beside them.

And when a woman like that feels threatened, she doesn't confront you directly…

    she cuts your legs out quietly.

This betrayal didn't feel like criticism.

It felt like abandonment.

It brought back all the same emotional echoes from my childhood.

The moment my mother told me to stop crying

The moment she chose my father to raise us

The moment I realized I could not trust adults to protect me

The moment my aunts walked away from my sister's scream

The pattern of women who didn't step in.

The pattern of women who protected themselves instead of the vulnerable.

It wasn't just a review.

It was another layer of:

"You're on your own."

"You misunderstood the relationship."

"Your trust was misplaced."

She wasn't just evaluating my work,

she was confirming a lifelong lesson:

Silence makes you easy to betray.

Betrayal in the workplace didn't end with a bad review.

It lingers.

It spreads.

It shapes the way others perceive you long after the ink dries on a document you never agreed to.

When she submitted that written review, the one that contradicted every word she had spoken to me, the fallout reached far beyond my feelings. It carried professional consequences that touched every part of my career.

And the worst part?

No one questioned it.

Not because it was true, but because it was easy.

Every company claims they evaluate employees holistically, but in reality, a single negative review can shadow you for years.

Her words became more.

A question mark next to my name.

A whisper in rooms I wasn't invited into.

A justification to pass me over.

A convenient weapon for anyone looking to undermine me.

A paper trail that didn't match the work I did every day.

And once something is in writing, corporate culture treats it as truth,

even when it was never spoken.

The review wasn't feedback.

It was framing.

She framed me.

And people believed the frame.

Before her betrayal, I was on a strong trajectory, recognition, promotions, stretch work, visibility.

After it?

Doors that had been open quietly swung shut.

Projects I would normally lead were handed to others.

Meetings I used to be invited to no longer included my name.

Leadership roles floated over my head as if I were invisible.

My work was still needed,

    but my growth was suddenly negotiable.

And no one said it out loud,

    but I knew the reason.

That review had redefined me without my consent.

The corporate world is a game of hierarchy and perception.

The moment one leader labels you as "less than,"

    others take it as an invitation to adjust their behavior.

I started noticing shifts.

People stopped asking for my input.

People assumed I lacked capability.

People talked over me more.

People dismissed my ideas before hearing them.

People treated me like I needed supervision instead of respect.

Even those who knew I was competent began treating me cautiously, as
    if they were waiting to see whether she was right.

And that is how one lie becomes a culture.

The hardest part wasn't losing opportunities.

It was losing trust.

I lost trust in:

HR processes,

leadership fairness,

women in power,

documentation that claimed to be "objective",

the illusion of meritocracy,

the belief that honesty protects you,

the idea that good work speaks for itself.

I did good work.

I gave everything.

I delivered consistently.

I took on tasks no one wanted.

I supported my team.

I stayed late.

I met impossible deadlines.

And none of that mattered when one person decided to rewrite my narrative.

It made me walk on eggshells, again.

Childhood taught me to scan for danger.

Her betrayal brought that survival skill roaring back.

I found myself:

> over-explaining,

> over-documenting,

> second-guessing every email,

> rehearsing every sentence in meetings,

> softening my voice to avoid sounding "threatening",

> volunteering for extra work to "prove" myself,

> staying late to avoid any perception of inadequacy.

I became a child again,

> careful, quiet, hyper-aware.

That's what betrayal does.

It resurrects old wounds in modern settings.

This part is important,

Even though the fallout was real, even though it cost me opportunities, time, advancement, and peace,

> *it did not define my future.*

It initiated me.

Into a different kind of leadership.

A different kind of strength.

A different relationship with women.

A different relationship with my own voice.

It dissolved the last remnants of the belief that silence would protect me.

It didn't break my career.

It refined my path.

It didn't destroy my trust.

It rerouted it to the people who deserved it.

It didn't weaken me.

It armored me.

And from this fallout came a deeper truth:

I wasn't meant to fit into their system.

I was meant to outgrow it.

Chapter 17: The Price of Boundaries

By this time in my life, I had survived broken homes, broken love, broken promises.

But nothing prepared me for the way the workplace could break me in a quieter, more polished way.

At least in childhood, the chaos was obvious.

In adulthood, the chaos wore a tie and sat in a meeting room.

I was working for a global company when a leader approached me about traveling to South America to support an audit.

It wasn't in my job description.

It wasn't part of my responsibilities.

And there was someone on the team,

    a woman from that country, fluent in the language,

    deeply embedded in the culture,

    who was far more qualified for the assignment.

But none of that mattered.

What mattered was this:

    He asked because he assumed I would say yes.

    Because women say yes.

    Because single mothers say yes, even when we shouldn't.

Because employees who don't want conflict say yes.

Because he believed his authority outweighed my reality.

But I said no.

A simple, reasonable, professional no.

I had a middle school child and two toddlers at home.

The assignment wasn't mine.

The qualified resource was right there.

I even offered support remotely.

It should have ended there.

It didn't.

He wrote me up.

Not for insubordination.

Not for poor performance.

Not for lack of skill.

But for "not being a team player."

Let that sit for a moment.

A woman with young children saying no to international travel, travel that wasn't required, relevant, or logical, was branded as difficult.

If I had said yes,

I would have been praised as flexible.

Dedicated.

Hard-working.

Committed.

Saying yes would have protected his ego.

Saying no protected my family.

And for that, I was punished.

It didn't stop at a write-up.

This leader weaponized his influence.

When another department wanted to hire me,

> when I had finally been offered a role that aligned with my career path,

> my ambition,

> my skill…he blocked the transfer.

Not because I wasn't qualified.

Not because the other team didn't want me.

But because he could.

He lobbied with another leader, together they placed me on an improvement plan. A tool meant for performance issues,

> not parenting responsibilities,

> not workload fairness,

not boundary setting.

Improvement plan.

For choosing my children.

For honoring my time.

For protecting my family.

For saying no to something unreasonable.

It was retaliation masquerading as procedure.

And the worst part?

He smiled when he did it.

That smug, quiet, self-satisfied smile

    of someone who believes they hold all the power.

The smile of a man who thinks silencing a woman is a victory.

The smile of someone who wanted me to know

    my boundaries inconvenienced him,

    and he would make sure I paid for it.

People see the write-up.

They see the blocked transfer.

They see the paper trail.

What they don't see is the psychological weight.

The frustration.

The helplessness.

The shame, even though I did nothing wrong.

The fear of being seen as "difficult."

The pressure to stay quiet.

This wasn't just a career setback.

It was a trigger.

A reminder of all the times adults ignored my needs.

All the times my voice didn't matter.

All the times I was punished for choosing myself.

All the times no one protected me.

All the times I was left to figure out survival alone.

This wasn't just workplace retaliation.

It was a reenactment of childhood,

    except now I finally recognized the pattern.

So…

I stayed.

I worked.

I delivered.

Even when it was unfair.

Even when it was insulting.

Even when he tried to push me out.

Even when the system backed him.

And slowly, quietly, systematically:

I outperformed his narrative.

He couldn't dismantle my competence.

The improvement plan faded.

His smugness faded.

His power over my career faded.

But I didn't.

They punish mothers for mothering.

They punish women for protecting their time.

They punish strong voices for saying "No."

They punish boundaries.

They punish autonomy.

They punish anything that is not blind compliance.

And women like me, women who survived childhoods where silence was survival, are expected to stay silent again.

But the storm inside me had grown too strong for that.

This wasn't the end of my career.

This is about more than one man.

It's about a system that trains women to:

overextend,

overwork,

overperform,

overcompensate,

overprove themselves.

Just to be seen as "enough."

It's about the way women with families are treated as liabilities.

It's about how boundaries are punished rather than respected.

And it's about how women rise anyway.

For the first time, I understood that.

I could say no.

I could stand my ground.

I could survive retaliation.

I could outlast unfair leaders.

I could protect my family and my career.

I could fight and win quietly.

I could be the kind of leader I needed when I was younger.

This chapter isn't about punishment.

It's about resilience.

It's about how I didn't just weather the storm,

I awoke it. Thunder, wind, lightning. I found my voice, hidden for so

long.

Chapter 18: The Early Arrival of Grief

Grief changes you, even when you don't have the language to understand what's happening.

And when it comes too early, as mine did, it can split your world in a way that you never fully recover.

I was a freshman in high school when I learned what death really meant.

Not the distant loss of someone old or expected.

Not the passing of a relative you're told you should love.

Not the ceremonial grief adults stage because it's appropriate.

This was different.

This was piercing.

Personal.

Unfair.

Wrong.

This was Chris.

He wasn't just a friend, he was part of my circle, my daily life, my laughter, my memories.

He was woven into the fabric of my teenage world in the way only adolescence allows intensely, fully, without boundaries.

And then, suddenly, he was gone.

I remember sitting in class that morning, bored, not thinking about anything in particular. Then the classroom door opened, and someone handed the teacher a slip of paper.

My name was called.

I felt that familiar jolt, 'What did I do? Am I in trouble?'

But when I walked into the counselor's office, everything froze.

I saw Ginny first,

    collapsed in a chair, crying so hard she couldn't breathe.

I had never seen her like that.

The counselor's voice was calm, too calm.

He said Chris's name.

He said the word "died."

I just stood there.

Still.

Silent.

Unable to move.

People talk about life "flashing before your eyes."

I always thought it sounded dramatic, exaggerated, something people said for effect.

But it's real.

It happens.

Every moment I had ever shared with him flickered through my mind in seconds.

The walking to class, jokes, notes passed in hallways, stupid arguments, summer days, secrets whispered in the way only teenagers whisper them, … ambrosia.

And then… nothing.

A void.

A blank space where a person used to be.

I didn't cry.

I didn't scream.

I didn't collapse.

I went still.

That was my training.

That was my conditioning.

Crying was a luxury I was never allowed.

Grieving was a performance I didn't know how to express.

Emotion was something you suppressed to avoid making others uncomfortable.

So, I froze,

    emotion trapped inside my body.

At home, grief was never nurtured.

It was managed.

Timed.

Dismissed.

So, when Chris died, I knew the rules:

> don't break down,

> don't burden anyone,

> don't make it a problem,

> don't feel too much.

When I finally made it home, I went to my room and collapsed into myself.

I cried, quietly, into a pillow, making sure no one heard.

But the next morning, my mother told me plainly:

> "Enough. Go to school. Stop this stupid behavior."

The words sliced through me.

Everything I felt was reduced to "stupid."

My loss was inconvenient.

My grief was excessive.

My pain was embarrassing her.

So, I shut it down.

Again.

And again.

I didn't cry for him after that.

That's what emotional conditioning does.

It teaches you how to grieve in silence,

>   how to hurt in private,

>   how to turn heartbreak into something you swallow.

I didn't just feel sad.

I felt guilty.

Did he know we loved him?

Could we have said something?

Could we have done something?

Did he think we wouldn't care?

Teenage brains are not equipped to process loss, especially not self-inflicted loss, especially not when the adults around them shut it down instead of holding space for it.

So, the guilt stayed.

Quietly.

Permanently.

It was one more weight I carried into adulthood.

Losing Chris at such a young age taught me things teenagers shouldn't have to learn.

That people can disappear without warning.

That someone can be laughing with you one week and gone the next.

That unresolved pain doesn't always make itself visible.

That adults can fail you in the moments you need them most.

That grief without support becomes a wound that never fully closes.

It also taught me.

A deeper understanding of life, it was fragile, unpredictable, and sometimes unbearably unfair.

But it also awakened a truth I didn't recognize until much later.

My heart felt deeply, even when I wasn't allowed to show it.

My grief was real, even when it wasn't acknowledged.

My love for others mattered, even when it wasn't validated.

This was the beginning of something important;

my emotional world was bigger than the silence I had been raised in.

Chris's death didn't just break my heart.

It cracked the numbness I had built to survive.

I did just that. I survived.

That is, until I heard the words saying *she's gone*.

Her name was Jodi.

She was my friend, my sister.

I loved her.

I was going to be there for her, like a big sister, no matter what life threw at her.

And life threw a lot.

A painful divorce.

A struggle with alcohol.

A loneliness that felt bottomless.

I welcomed her into my home, held her hand through recovery, celebrated when she found the man of her dreams and remarried.

We talked until we cried, laughed until our stomachs hurt.

She was family, the kind you choose.

But as with most adult lives, life gets in the way.

Distance grows in the spaces between phone calls.

Business becomes an excuse.

And Hector, making it difficult to chat with her.

And Jodi started to tumble in silence.

I didn't know.

But she was already slipping away, and I was too wrapped in my own survival to notice her drowning.

I didn't see the cracks widening until it was too late.

I called and called, asked to see her, to feed our souls with carbs, sweets, and conversation. Anything for her to take my call.

Then, one day, she was just… gone.

Alone, in a hotel room.

Sad and misunderstood.

But I *did* understand.

And I wanted her back.

This grief was different from the one I carried for Chris.

With Jodi, I grieved a love I had failed to protect.

With Jodi, I was just another person who couldn't stop the rain.

Jodi's storm sucked her into its wind tunnel, and then it left as the sun went down.

This time, the grief was powerful.

I didn't silence it.

I didn't swallow it.

I didn't let anyone tell me it was "stupid" or that I should "get over it."

This time, I let it live.

And grief *does* live.

It doesn't fade.

It doesn't disappear.

It moves in, unpacks its bags, and learns the layout of your heart.

It erupts in a Jason's Deli at lunchtime, tears flooding into a potato, in a room full of strangers who stopped chewing to ask if I'm okay.

One woman, a virtual stranger, held my hand and prayed, for Jodi, for me, for all of us who miss people we can't bring back.

And in that moment, grief wasn't a burden.

It was a bridge.

It connected me to humanity in a way I had never been given before.

Then, in that moment, an almost virtual stranger became a guide.

He didn't fix me. He held my quaking shoulders riveted by the sobs.

He witnessed me.

And in being witnessed, I began to understand.

Grief is not something you survive.

It's something you carry.

And sometimes, it carries you, right into the arms of someone kind enough to say, *I see you. It's okay to hurt.*

I realized then that all the grief I had ever silenced for Chris, for my childhood, for the mother I needed but didn't have, for the father who couldn't love me safely, hadn't actually gone away.

It had been waiting.

Waiting for me to be ready to feel it.

Waiting for me to understand that grief isn't the enemy.

Silence is.

With Jodi, I finally let grief breathe.

And in breathing, it began to change.

It became less about pain and more about love.

Less about absence and more about presence. The presence of her memory, her impact, her place in my story.

She was gone, but my love for her wasn't.

And that love became a kind of light, a soft, enduring glow that no amount of darkness could completely extinguish.

This chapter wasn't about death, it was about acceptence:

Acceptance to grief,

Acceptance to love,

Acceptance to how deeply I could feel,

Acceptance to the truth that emotions are not weaknesses,

This is where something inside me whispered:

you are meant to feel,

you are meant to care,

you are meant for more than silence.

Part 3: Summary

This is the beginning of fractures in the walls.

The beginning of masks falling away.

The beginning of seeing who stands with me and who was never there.

It's about awareness of:

the smile that cuts deeper than any blade,

grief that arrives too early and stays too long,

the silence you were taught to call strength.

Now is the time to let grief move in, feel it, cry;

Time to stop swallowing my pain to make others comfortable.

Time to become the storm.

Part 4: Becoming the Storm

Every storm has an eye,

a still point,

a moment of clarity,

where the chaos pauses and you can finally see what has been rearranged.

This is the awakening.

The return.

The moment when the woman and the weather become one,

and the clearing sky is not an end, but a beginning.

Chapter 19: When Someone Finally Sees You

Not all storms come from men.

And not all shelter does either.

After years of working in male-dominated industries, construction, oil and gas, power, I had learned to navigate the environment like a second language.

I understood the jokes.

I understood the hierarchy.

I understood when to speak and when to stay quiet.

I understood how to blend in without making waves.

It wasn't that I didn't see the disrespect.

It was that I had adapted to survive it.

By then, I had been talked over, dismissed, subtly mocked, labeled difficult, passed over, targeted, and punished for boundaries more times than I could count.

I had normalized it;

> because normalizing harm is what you do when you've never been taught how to call it out.

But then I met someone who changed everything.

He didn't arrive as a savior; he arrived as a mirror.

He was just a coworker.

Someone competent.

Someone steady.

Someone who treated everyone on the team with fairness and respect.

He wasn't loud or political or performative.

He was simply observant,

and what he observed in meetings, he didn't like.

It started small.

One day after a meeting, he casually said:

"Did you notice how they dismissed your question without answering it?"

I hadn't.

Or maybe I had?

But I had buried it under the years of conditioning that taught me not to make it about me.

Another day:

"They lifted your idea and gave credit to someone else. That happens to you a lot."

And then:

"You know they interrupt you more than anyone else, right?"

I blinked.

I froze.

I didn't know what to say.

Because for the first time in my professional life, someone wasn't questioning my perception —

they were validating it.

He wasn't confused.

He wasn't minimizing.

He wasn't debating.

He wasn't telling me to calm down or take it less personally.

He was saying,

"I saw it too."

And that was everything.

His observations were gentle, not preachy.

Objective, not emotional.

Almost like someone quietly handing you a pair of glasses,

and the world comes into focus for the first time.

Once he pointed out the patterns,

I couldn't unsee them.

The way leaders asked me to justify things no one else had to justify.

The way men repeated my ideas minutes later as if they were theirs.

The way decisions were made in hallways, not meetings.

The way people softened their tone with men but sharpened it with me.

The way my expertise was questioned but my labor was relied upon.

The way my boundaries were challenged while others' were respected.

The way I was held to higher expectations but given fewer resources.

The way I was expected to absorb more work without complaint.

It wasn't paranoia.

It wasn't insecurity.

It wasn't "in my head."

It was real.

And now, someone else had the courage and integrity to say it.

It wasn't just validation;

    it was a disruption.

For the first time in my career,

    a man wasn't defending the system.

He wasn't making excuses for it.

He wasn't trying to smooth it over.

He wasn't benefitting from my silence.

He was breaking the pattern.

Because male-dominated environments don't change

when women complain —

they change when men start paying attention.

And he paid attention.

He paid attention when I was interrupted.

He paid attention when I was talked over.

He paid attention when I wasn't given credit.

He paid attention when I was held to impossible standards.

He paid attention when leadership used condescension instead of collaboration.

He saw what I had been conditioned to tolerate.

And he named it.

Not to "save" me, but to empower me.

That was the difference.

He didn't need to fix anything.

He didn't need to speak for me.

He didn't need to make grand gestures.

He simply stood beside me in ways that mattered:

He redirected conversations back to me when people talked over me.

He gave me credit in meetings where others tried to claim my work.

He challenged leaders when they dismissed my expertise.

He amplified my voice when others tried to minimize it.

He validated my boundaries.

He treated me like a peer, not a subordinate.

He made room for me in spaces where others tried to squeeze me out.

He didn't change the culture,

    but he changed my experience inside it.

He didn't solve everything,

    but he made me feel less alone.

And sometimes, that is all you need

    to start reclaiming your power.

This wasn't romantic.

This wasn't emotional dependency.

This wasn't rescue.

This was recognition.

Something I had rarely received from any man in my personal or professional life.

He saw the patterns,

    and reflected them back to me

    without distortion, ego, or agenda.

For the first time, someone treated me the way I treated others,

    with honesty, respect, and care.

And it woke something inside me.

I began to trust my own perceptions more than the gaslighting around me.

I began to expect respect instead of hoping for it.

I began to speak up more boldly.

I began to take up more space.

I began to lead with confidence instead of caution.

He didn't create my strength.

He mirrored it.

He didn't empower me.

He reminded me of the power I already had.

This chapter isn't about a man,

    it's about recognition

Recognition changes things.

When someone finally sees you,

    the real you,

    the capable you,

    the intelligent you,

the intuitive you —

The world shifts.

Not because they gave you permission,

    but because they reflected back the truth you had always known.

You are not imagining it.

You are not overreacting.

You are not the problem.

You are not too much.

You are not too sensitive.

You are not "difficult."

You are a woman in a system not built for you,

    and you are rising anyway.

Being believed didn't make me loud.

It made me clear.

Being supported didn't make me dependent.

It made me stronger.

Being seen didn't make me arrogant.

It made me unapologetic.

This was where I finally understood:

I didn't need approval.

I needed allies.

I needed people who valued truth over comfort.

I needed people who treated me like I deserved to be there,
    because I did.

The storm inside me was no longer a quiet, internal thing.

It was forceful and had purpose.

An awakening.

A reclaiming.

A rising.

This chapter isn't about the good man.

It's about the woman he helped me remember I already was.

Chapter 20: Motherhood, Rewritten

Becoming a mother did not just change my life,

    it changed me.

It rewrote the way I saw the world,

    the way I understood love,

    the way I held pain,

    and the way I defined strength.

But perhaps the greatest shift of all was this:

    motherhood awakened the woman I was always meant to be,

    not the woman I was conditioned to become.

For the first time in my life,

I wasn't surviving for myself.

I was surviving, and rising,

for three little souls who deserved better than the storms I grew up in.

And somewhere along the way,

    they helped me become a woman

    who finally believed she deserved better too.

I became the mother I needed as a child.

Nothing prepares you for motherhood,

but everything prepares you to mother the way you choose.

I knew exactly what I didn't want to be.

A mother who silenced emotions.

A mother who weaponized shame.

A mother who ignored pain.

A mother who chose convenience over care.

A mother who dismissed the hearts she was responsible for securing.

A mother who let chaos go unspoken.

A mother who kept secrets instead of offering safety.

I knew what it felt like to be unseen.

So I try to make sure my children are seen.

I knew what it felt like to carry burdens alone.

So I made space for their burdens,

    so they never had to hide in the dark like their mom.

I knew what it felt like to fear expressing needs.

So I taught, and teach, my children to speak,

    even when their voices shook.

I knew what it felt like to be expected to be "fine."

So I let them be human. I let them feel the pain, and I held them.

And slowly... something miraculous happened.

As I learned how to raise them,

I learned how to re-raise myself.

My children became mirrors, reflecting the truth I had not known.

There's something disarming about children.

They don't see your history.

They don't see your scars.

They see your essence.

They see your softness.

Your humor.

Your intelligence.

Your curiosity.

Your spirit.

Your goodness, even when you don't.

For decades, I had seen myself through the eyes of adults who hurt me,

    partners who undervalued me,

        and workplaces that underestimated me.

But my children saw the truth.

They saw a mother who fought for them.

Who provided for them.

Who protected them.

Who didn't give up.

Who didn't break.

Who carried responsibility, even when it was heavy.

Who gave love freely, even when she, I, had never received it.

They saw a hero I never knew I was.

And in seeing myself through their eyes,

I began to believe I was worthy of the same compassion I gave them.

When my son came home from college,

>   he didn't just return as my son.

He returned as a guide.

Gentle.

Centered.

Philosophical.

Emotionally mature in a way that felt both familiar and surprising.

He reminded me of things I used to believe in,

>   before life hardened me,

>   before survival became my default mode.

He said things like:

>   "Mom, everything works out if you let it."

>   "Don't fight what's not meant for you."

"You don't need to prove your worth."

"The world isn't punishing you. It's redirecting you."

"You can rest."

His words unlocked something,

a softness I had forgotten how to access.

He showed me peace.

The kind of peace I had been denied my entire childhood,

The kind of peace I never believed I was allowed to feel.

My daughters taught me how to be brave and soft at the same time.

My girls came into the world like fireflies,

small, bright lights with an inherent magic.

Mothering daughters after the storms of my past

was a sacred responsibility.

I didn't want them to inherit:

my fear,

my silence,

my self-doubt,

my patterns,

my wounds,

my shrinking.

So, I changed how I raised them.

I encouraged independence.

I encouraged curiosity.

I encouraged boundaries, real ones.

I encouraged self-expression, even when it was inconvenient.

I encouraged emotional honesty.

I encouraged them to take up space, loudly, boldly, unapologetically.

But here's the part I never expected.

In teaching them to be brave, I learned bravery myself.

In teaching them to set boundaries, I began setting my own.

In teaching them their worth, I finally acknowledged mine.

They taught me how softness was not weakness.

It was a strength I didn't know how to access.

Every generation has a breaking point.

A moment where a woman decides,

   this ends with me.

The silence ends with me.

The shame ends with me.

The neglect ends with me.

The fear ends with me.

The generational pain ends with me.

I was that woman.

Motherhood gave me the courage to stop the cycle,

to rewrite the script I had been given,

to walk away from the molds that harmed me,

to refuse the roles society tried to cage me in.

I didn't raise my children in the shadow of my trauma.

I raised them in the light of my healing.

Motherhood didn't heal every wound.

But it opened the door.

It showed me:

what love can look like,

what safety can feel like,

what boundaries can protect,

what presence can nurture,

what emotional intelligence can create,

And ultimately,

motherhood became the catalyst,

for becoming the woman I needed all along.

Not perfect.

Not unscarred.

Not untouched by pain.

But whole.

Awake.

Evolving.

Unapologetic.

This is where healing shifted from survival

to transformation.

This is where the storm realized

she carries sunlight too!.

Chapter 21: Returning to Myself

Some truths never leave you.

Even when life pulls you away from them.

Even when circumstances bury them.

Even when responsibilities drown them out.

Purpose doesn't disappear.

It waits.

It waited for me through childhood storms.

It waited through young love and heartbreak.

It waited through motherhood and survival.

It waited through workplace betrayals and career roadblocks.

It waited while I built a life that looked stable from the outside but felt misaligned on the inside.

And eventually, after years of noise,

 of chaos,

 of endurance,

 the waiting was over.

My purpose began calling me back.

I was always meant for healing, I just didn't know how to claim it.

Back in college, before life demanded survival over dreams,

I found a field that lit something inside me:

    psychoneuroimmunology.

It was the first time anything had made complete sense to me.

Stress imprints itself in the bloodstream.

Trauma reshapes the brain.

Thoughts change physiology.

Healing is not just emotional,

    it's biological.

It connected everything I had lived through.

The loneliness that settled into my bones.

The silence that created anxiety I couldn't name.

The pressure that lived in my chest for years.

The exhaustion that never felt like "just being tired."

The way my body remembered things I tried to forget.

It explained why I felt older than my age,

    why my system ran on high alert,

    why I survived things I shouldn't have survived.

I was meant to study wellness.

I was meant to heal.

I was meant to help others break the cycles they didn't even know they were trapped in.

But life had other demands.

And I did what I had always done,

   I put myself second.

My dreams were deferred.

But they were not erased.

After everything I'd lived through, something began to wake.

It didn't happen all at once.

It began quietly, the way storms often do.

A thought I couldn't shake.

A memory of the work I once wanted to do.

A curiosity I felt tugging in my chest.

A sense that something was missing —

   not from my life, but from me.

Leaving the toxic job lit the first spark.

Finally stepping away from a controlling relationship lit the second.

Raising children who were taught to speak their truth lit the third.

And then something unexpected happened.

The man who held my tears in the middle of Jason's Deli, not a lover, not a rescuer, but someone who reminded me of myself.

A friend.

A colleague.

A gentle mirror.

Someone who talked openly about wellness, intuition, energy, alignment, meaning.

Someone who wasn't afraid to question the grind.

Someone who introduced me to the possibility that I could rediscover the girl I left behind in college.

He didn't heal me,

    he reminded me I could heal myself.

He helped me remember.

I wasn't broken.

I was buried.

And now it was time to unearth the woman underneath.

I started reading again.

Books on energy.

Books on the nervous system.

Books on trauma, resilience, healing.

I found myself drawn to things that had always made sense to me:

meditation,

movement,

natural wellness,

emotional awareness,

the mind-body connection.

The things I once thought I needed a degree to practice,

I realized I had been practicing internally for years.

And then I began to feel something new.

Peace.

Not the kind that comes from stillness,

but the kind that comes from alignment.

The kind that whispers:

"This is who you are."

"This is what you were meant to do."

"This is the calling life tried to take from you."

"And it's not too late."

When my son came home from college, he had changed,

not in personality,

but in presence.

He was calmer.

More grounded.

More spiritually aware.

More aligned with his own intuition.

He reminded me of things I used to believe in college, the space where I could exist just as me, without the family, without the influence.

Just my own thoughts.

Defining my own beliefs.

What I believed was:

    everything has meaning,

    alignment matters,

    life works for us, not against us,

    fear isn't truth,

    rest is productive,

    we deserve to feel whole.

He told me not to worry.

He told me everything would work out.

He told me I deserved more ease, more joy, more purpose.

He wasn't just my son,

    he was my sign.

A symbol of what happens when generational patterns break.

A reminder that healing is not linear.

He helped bring me home to myself.

I began breaking the mold, not just for me, but for my children.

The mold my parents created for me:

    the mold of silence,

    the mold of self-sacrifice,

    the mold of emotional suppression,

    the mold of survival without thriving.

I started smashing it.

I wanted to allow my kids to feel.

To explore.

To speak.

To question.

To become who they were meant to be.

To do this, I had to do the same things for myself.

Though I am still learning, I had to start to:

    prioritize rest,

    reconnect with my body,

    nurture my intuition,

explore healing practices,

listen to my inner voice,

release guilt,

welcome softness.

I began to feel something I had not felt since early childhood.

My own presence. My own mind.

My own desires. My own power.

My own self.

It was time to reclaim my life.

For decades, I had lived according to other people's expectations:

parents, partners, bosses, systems, culture.

Now, I was learning to live according to my own.

This was the beginning of:

autonomy,

identity,

purpose,

wholeness.

I wasn't trying to be loved.

I wasn't trying to belong.

I wasn't trying to earn approval.

I was becoming someone I had almost forgotten.

The girl who believed healing was possible.

The woman who knew she was meant to guide others.

The storm who learned she could calm herself.

This chapter is the beginning of my reclamation,

    my return to the woman I abandoned,

    because the world forced me to.

But I didn't lose her. She waited for me.

And now, I am finally returning to her,

    with the strength,

    with wisdom,

    with the resilience and clarity,

    that only a woman who has weathered every kind of storm can carry.

Chapter 22: Breaking the Mold

There comes a moment when you look at everything you have survived, everything you have built, everything you have sacrificed and realize,

none of this reflects who I truly am.

It reflects who I had to be.

For years, my identity had been shaped by the roles the world assigned me.

The daughter who survived chaos.

The child who stayed silent.

The teenager who complied.

The young woman who endured.

The partner who carried the weight.

The employee who worked twice as hard.

The mother who kept everyone afloat.

I played the parts well because I had no choice.

The mold that shaped me was built from:

my parents' wounds,

my childhood silencing,

societal roles handed to women,

trauma disguised as responsibility,

workplaces designed to keep women small,

relationships that fed on my empathy,

cultural scripts about what women should endure.

The mold told me to:

be quiet,

be agreeable,

be responsible for everyone,

be resilient instead of supported,

be the one who adjusts,

be the one who gives,

be the one who explains,

be the one who forgives,

be the one who stays.

But I started to see more clearly.

The mold wasn't built to help me.

It was built to contain me.

And containers are not homes.

Breaking the mold wasn't a single explosion,

it was a series of cracks that spread until I could no longer fit inside.

The first crack came the day I realized I didn't trust my marriage.

The second, when I left a toxic job.

The third, when my son showed me I deserved peace.

The fourth, when a coworker validated the disrespect I had normalized.

The fifth, when I remembered the girl who loved science and healing.

The sixth, when I watched my children grow and blossom without shrinking.

Every crack was a reminder.

The woman I had been isn't the woman I wanted to be.

The mold had shaped me, but it no longer defined me.

People imagine transformation as wild and cinematic.

Mine wasn't.

My breakthrough was,

    choosing truth over tradition,

    choosing boundaries over approval,

    choosing wellness over burnout,

    choosing authenticity over performance,

    choosing myself over the roles others wanted me to play.

Breaking the mold looks like:

    saying no without guilt,

    saying yes without permission,

not apologizing for my tone,

refusing to explain my choices,

refusing to tolerate disrespect,

letting go of relationships that drain me,

demanding equity at work,

taking up space in conversations,

advocating for my children and myself,

trusting my worth.

Breaking the mold isn't about becoming someone new,

it was about remembering the woman I was always meant to be.

For the first time, I didn't measure my value by

the hours I worked,

the projects I completed,

the crises I fixed,

the praise I received,

the promotions I was denied.

Instead, I measure my value by:

how honest I could be,

how aligned I felt internally,

how safely my team could speak with me,

how much peace I brought into my home,

how authentically I could lead with compassion and strength.

I stopped performing.

I started becoming.

This shift changed everything,

not overnight, but undeniably.

I stopped trying to be the perfect mother.

Instead, I became an honest one.

And my home is changing.

The air feels lighter.

My children feel freer.

I feel more myself than I have in years.

I am not raising them in reaction to my own past anymore.

I am raising them from a place of healing.

Breaking the mold isn't the end.

It's the *Beginning*

When you break a mold,

you don't become shapeless.

You become self-shaped.

I no longer needed to:

fit a role,

earn love,

justify my worth,

negotiate my boundaries,

make myself small.

I had stepped outside the expectations placed on me,

and found a life that finally matched the woman I was becoming.

This wasn't rebellion. It was reclamation.

Not destruction, but reconstruction.

Not chaos, but clarity.

When I broke the mold,

I discovered something extraordinary.

I wasn't fragile clay meant to be shaped by others.

I was the hands.

I was the fire.

I was the sculptor of my own life.

And the storm building inside me my entire life was no longer something to fear.

It was finally something I could use.

There is a moment of acknowledgment - after years of surviving, enduring, fighting, healing, rising - when a woman looks at her life and finally recognizes herself.

Not the self the world shaped.

Not the self others demanded.

Not the self she performed to stay safe.

Her true self.

The one who was always there, buried beneath survival.

This is that moment.

Chapter 23: Storms

People assume storms appear suddenly.

They don't.

They build.

They form from pressure, from heat, from imbalance, from the friction between what is expected and what is true.

They grow quietly at first,

> in the corners of childhood homes,

> in the silence of emotional suppression,

> in the confusion of blurred boundaries,

> in the heartbreaks that cleave you open,

> in the workplaces that undervalue you,

> in the relationships that shrink you,

> in the moments you compromise yourself to keep the peace.

Storms do not appear out of nowhere.

They develop in the women who have endured too much yet still rise anyway.

I didn't set out to become a storm.

But life forged one inside me.

I am no longer what happened to me. I am what I became after it all.

I am what I created from the devastation left by the storm.

A storm is not a sign of chaos.

It is a sign of change.

It clears what no longer belongs.

It reshapes landscapes.

It exposes foundations.

It brings renewal.

I broke the mold.

I shattered the patterns.

I rewrote the script.

I am not small anymore.

I am not quiet.

I am not contained.

I have outgrown every version of myself shaped by survival.

There is strength in naming what happened.

There is power in breaking generational patterns.

There is healing in choosing differently.

There is liberation in stepping into your truth.

But the ultimate transformation is realizing,

you don't owe your past any more space.

You owe your future everything.

I owe myself a life that feels good.

And I will have it,

    because I have become the force that creates it.

And this is only the beginning.

Part 4: Summary

The storm is not the end of my story.

It is the beginning of the life I was always meant to live.

Because after everything I have weathered,

everything I have endured,

everything I have rebuilt…

I am not afraid of storms.

I am the Storm.

A Letter: To the Woman Still Navigating the Weather

To the woman reading this who still feels trapped inside the weather,

I see you.

Not the version of you that the world sees —

> the polished one, the strong one, the capable one who keeps everything together.

I see the woman underneath that armor.

The woman who holds too much.

The woman who wonders if she will ever feel safe, or whole, or enough.

You may not know this yet,

> but you are already surviving storms you haven't even named.

You are already stronger than you realize.

You are already carrying wisdom inside you that life hasn't fully revealed.

So let me tell you what I wish someone had told me.

There is nothing wrong with you.

There is nothing broken in you.

There is nothing unworthy about you.

You are not dramatic.

You are not too emotional.

You are not imagining it.

You are not asking for too much.

You are simply a woman who has weathered more than most will ever understand,

and you are ***still standing***.

That alone is extraordinary.

If you are still silencing yourself,

I understand.

You learned to stay quiet to stay safe.

You learned to carry burdens so others didn't have to.

You learned to smile through discomfort,

to soothe the feelings of people who never protected yours,

to put your own needs last.

But hear me now:

Your voice matters.

Your emotions matter.

Your needs matter.

You are allowed to take up space.

You are allowed to say no.

You are allowed to change.

You are allowed to walk away.

You are allowed to want more.

You are allowed to rest.

You are allowed to unlearn everything that hurt you.

You are allowed to choose yourself.

If you are still in relationships that make you shrink,

I understand.

I stayed too long in places where my worth was rationed.

I rationalized red flags.

I confused intensity with love.

I confused obligation with commitment.

I believed that endurance was the measure of devotion.

But the truth is simple:

Love is never meant to cost you yourself.

If you must disappear to keep someone else comfortable,

that is not love, that is captivity.

You deserve a love that sees you.

A love that holds you without dimming you.

A love that feels like freedom, not fear.

If you are still in workplaces that undervalue you,

I understand.

I stood in rooms where my insight was ignored and my labor was taken for granted.

Where boundaries were punished,

where motherhood was treated as a liability,

where powerful women mimicked oppressive men,

and where my quiet competence was exploited instead of celebrated.

And still, I rose.

You will too.

You deserve spaces where your voice is not only heard,

but sought out.

Where your work is not only seen,

but recognized.

Where your strength is not feared,

but respected.

Do not dim yourself to make others comfortable.

If you are still haunted by your past,

I understand.

Childhood teaches us things we spend adulthood unlearning.

Silence.

Fear.

Guilt.

Hyper-independence.

Self-doubt.

Distorted definitions of love.

But *your past is not your prison.*

The things that happened to you

    do not define what is possible for you.

Healing is not about forgetting.

It is about reclaiming.

And you are allowed to reclaim everything they tried to take from you:

Your voice.

Your body.

Your boundaries.

Your intuition.

Your dreams.

Your self-worth.

Your future.

If you are still inside your storm,

I want you to know this:

You are not lost.

You are transforming.

Storms are not signs of failure.

They are signs of change.

You are shedding old versions of yourself.

You are breaking harmful patterns.

You are confronting truths others ran from.

You are building strength in places that once collapsed.

You are reshaping your entire life,

even if you don't see it yet.

Storms are messy, chaotic, loud, blinding.

But they are also cleansing.

Clarifying.

Powerful.

Necessary.

And when the rain stops,

and it will,

you won't just walk out of the storm.

You will walk out as the storm.

Not because you are destructive.

But because you are unstoppable.

Not because you tear things down.

But because you build new worlds.

Not because you're fierce for the sake of fear.

But because you are finally alive in your truth.

So, to the woman still inside the weather,

Hold on.

Not because you must endure, but because you are evolving.

Not because you owe anyone anything, but because you owe yourself everything.

Not because you are weak, but because you are becoming whole.

You are not meant to survive your storm;

you are meant to become it.

And when you do,

when you step into the fullness of who you are,

when you allow yourself to be powerful without apology…

The world will open for you in ways it never could before.

You will not just rewrite your story.

You will write an entirely new ending.

And I promise you,

it's beautiful.

With love,

With fire,

With truth,

With the strength of every storm you've survived,

Krisi

The Healing Earth

If you are interested in learning how to reclaim yourself, I am available as a coach or as a speaker.

My books can be found at *KrisiRodriguez.com*.

My services and herbal products are available at *TheHealingEarthWellness.com*.

You are not alone. So many of us women have experienced similar triggers and know how you feel, even when you think they don't.

Smiles cover the pain.

Things are always different from what you think when the doors to the home close.

Reach out if you need help, please. You have friends, you just don't know their names yet!

Resources: Parenting is Hard

For me, knowing the right words and the right tone was difficult.

Talking to your children, to raise them with confidence in their emotions, can feel uncomfortable.

I was introduced to a book with pre-thought-out questions to help guide the conversation. It is gentle and encouraging for children.

It shows compassion,

Love,

Understanding.

Though it is written for young children,

It helps you think about the words and tone,

No matter what age.

I hope it helps.

Jayden's Big Feelings by Anthony Adams

Jayden's Big Feelings Adventures: Adams, Anthony: 9798276681870: Amazon.com: Books